# *Parenting by*
# DESIGN

# Parenting by
# DESIGN

## Discovering God's Original
## Design for Your Family

*Chris and Michelle Groff
with Lee Long*

WESTBOW°
PRESS
A DIVISION OF THOMAS NELSON
& ZONDERVAN

WestBow Press books may be ordered through booksellers or by contacting:

WestBow Press
A Division of Thomas Nelson & Zondervan
1663 Liberty Drive
Bloomington, IN 47403
www.westbowpress.com
1 (866) 928-1240

ISBN: 978-1-4908-3184-8 (sc)
ISBN: 978-1-4908-3185-5 (hc)
ISBN: 978-1-4908-3183-1 (e)

Library of Congress Control Number: 2014906163

Printed in the United States of America.

WestBow Press rev. date: 04/03/2014

# CONTENTS

# INTRODUCTION

## Chris Groff

God's plan can take us in unexpected directions. In 2003, my wife, Michelle, and I thought we had life under control. We were living a very comfortable lifestyle in Fort Worth, Texas, with our two sons. With financial security, lots of friends, and many of the best material possessions, we had no plans to change. But that summer, our lives took a radical turn that included drug addiction, a financial collapse, health issues, and eventually the loss of the lifestyle we had worked so hard to create. It was a perfect storm of what our culture would consider terrible losses, and we wouldn't wish those kinds of events on anyone else. But looking back on those years, we realize that God wasn't punishing us for drifting away from Him and into a self-indulgent lifestyle. He was saving us from ourselves. And it may sound weird, but we wouldn't trade any of those terrible times to regain what we lost. God used our difficulties to clear our path back to Him and give us a new mission.

Through a dramatic series of events, we were introduced to therapist Lee Long, and over time, Lee, Michelle, and I were led to start a ministry called Parenting by Design. The first Parenting by Design seminar series was held in Fort Worth in 2004, and since then we have had the privilege of teaching thousands of parents through live presentations, DVDs, audios, devotionals, an interactive website, and social media. The principles taught by Parenting by Design were developed by studying the Bible, through our personal experiences, by analyzing the latest research, and from years of working with all types of parents going through the challenging adventure of raising children.

This book is a joint effort by the three of us to compile what we've learned. For the sake of readability and flow, it is written in my voice, with Michelle and Lee contributing examples and illustrations from their points of view. Our prayer is that this book will help strengthen and encourage you in your efforts to raise your children according to God's design and with His help.

# CHAPTER 1

# OUR SON WAS A DRUG ADDICT?

One summer night in 2003, Michelle and I woke up suddenly to the ringing of the doorbell. I glanced at the clock. *Two thirty in the morning.* My anxiety rose as I raced through the possibilities. Were some kids playing a prank? Had one of our sons been in a car wreck? Was a neighbor in trouble?

I stumbled down the stairs, hoping it was just a minor annoyance. But when I opened the door, a friend of mine and his sixteen-year-old son were waiting on the front porch. Nothing could have prepared me for the story they proceeded to tell.

Stunned, I listened as they described catching my youngest son, Bob, and another kid attempting to steal the stereo system out of the friend's car. All I could think was *How could this be?* Bob had recently been elected to the high school honor council. He was a good student whose grades usually landed him on the honor roll. The only trouble he had ever gotten into was minor, and we had no reason to think it had gone this far. The kid they described didn't sound like our son.

But there was more. They told of Bob's drug use and other criminal activity. And just like that, Pandora's box had been opened.

I shut the door and walked back up the stairs. I had to tell Michelle.

Her reaction was a mixture of astonishment and fear and then skepticism. Surely, this was a monumental case of mistaken identity.

I called Bob on his cell phone. When he answered, I recounted what I had been told moments ago. He seemed as shocked as we were and vehemently denied the accusations.

"Okay, Bob," I said. "I'm on my way to pick you up."

When I pulled up to the friend's home where Bob was spending the night, he was outside waiting. He got into the car and tried to convince me that he was a falsely accused victim. But inconsistencies in his story quickly surfaced. And as his house of cards tumbled down, I could no longer escape the truth. Our worst fears had been confirmed. Bob had been leading a secret life that we were just uncovering. As he revealed more of his story, we knew we had a huge problem on our hands.

By the next morning, Michelle and I began to question ourselves. How could this have happened? We had never abused or neglected our kids. (Bob has a brother, Ben, who is almost two years older.) We loved them and had been very involved in their lives. Our boys lacked for nothing. We enrolled them in the best schools, made sure they had the latest toys and games, bought them cars when they turned sixteen, and took them on incredible vacations. We did everything we could think of to make them happy. We considered ourselves a "successful" family, at least in the way the world defines "success." Clearly, this disaster did not fit the script we had carefully crafted for our lives. We were dumbfounded.

Michelle and I knew we had to do something drastic, and we had to do it quickly. But we had no idea *what* to do. Obviously, the problem had escalated far beyond our control. We were sure Bob needed to get out of Fort Worth and into a recovery program where they could work with him twenty-four/seven, but finding the right place was a challenge. After a lot of soul-searching and some research by Michelle's sister Cynthia, we found a treatment program in Colorado where Bob would spend the next ten months—his entire junior year of high school. We dropped him off at the facility on July 17, 2003. It was one of the worst days of our lives.

Michelle and I were believers at the time, having trusted Christ long before, but we had drifted away from Him. Our affluence, with the attendant increase in our lifestyle, had made us proud, materialistic, and self-centered. We were focused on the things our culture told us were important: money, power, beauty, and fame. And to be honest, we had been rather successful in acquiring those things. This is humbling to admit, but that sense of self-sufficiency was part of why this event really shook us to the core. This wasn't supposed to happen to *us*.

When we accepted the fact that a big change was needed in Bob's life, we debated whether a thirty-day or ninety-day program would be enough to "fix" him or if he needed a longer program. The words of an admission director at a Christian facility resonated in our hearts. She said, "Many kids can change their outward behavior in three months, but it takes a lot longer to change the heart." While we were not spiritually focused at the time, we could see the wisdom of an approach based on heart-level change. Deep down, we knew Christ was the answer to our son's issues, and it didn't take us long to enroll him in this long-term, faith-based program. We were on our way to Colorado in a matter of days.

Bob's treatment program included family weekends in the fall and spring. These weekends gave the therapists who worked with the kids an opportunity to work with the parents to improve their parenting skills and prepare them for the children's return home. The therapists knew their work could be in vain if the child was sent back to the same dysfunctional home. But God was also working on our relationship with Him. Through this series of short parenting classes, Michelle and I—a couple of independent, worldly parents brought to their knees by this disaster—got reacquainted with God. In His perfect timing, He comforted us with a compassion that we just knew was coming from Him.

Michelle and I did not send our son to Colorado with an expectation that *we* would encounter God's love. But He was there, and it was the perfect time to draw us back to Him. The changes in our lives weren't instantaneous, but over the next months, we found ourselves turning to God over and over and finding true love and comfort. While I wouldn't wish what happened to us on anyone, I wouldn't trade that experience for anything. It led us back to our Creator and to a ministry that has given us the opportunity to encourage other parents.

Our experience at our son's treatment facility in Colorado caused us to think about parenting in a new way. We realized that our parenting methods—rather standard for a typical American family—were far more influenced by the world than by God. We began to understand that the way God parents us should be our guide for parenting our children and that God uses our parenting experiences to teach us more about Him. Looking back, we realized God doesn't waste an experience. He used our son's troubles to teach our whole family about His redemptive power and love.

During the ten months Bob was in the treatment program, his therapist, Lee Long, encouraged us to adopt a new attitude toward family communication and to try some new parenting practices. We learned a lot about asking open-ended questions, practicing reflective listening, letting experiences and consequences teach our kids, and empathizing with struggles. We had assumed that parents who loved their kids as much as we did would instinctively know how to be good parents, but that wasn't the case. The truth is we had not done a great job of teaching either of our sons how to be responsible decision makers, and we had fallen into common traps. When we started implementing the principles we were learning, the relational dynamic around our house began to change. In some respects, things got worse before they got better as our boys tried to push us back into our old, predictable parenting styles. But authentic communication slowly began to develop between our boys and us.

This required us to learn to be better listeners. Sadly, most of our past communication was a tug-of-war of opinions as we attempted to "correct" our kids' feelings and convince them to agree with our point of view. Guess what. They resisted our efforts! We realized that we had been trying to force our kids to conform to our design for their lives.

Making changes took us out of our comfort zone. Parents are supposed to talk and kids are supposed to listen, right? But in all of our lectures and nagging, we lost track of who *God* designed our kids to be. This new mode of communication required us to ask questions to uncover their unique God-given personalities and perspectives rather than trying to simply mold them into the people *we* wanted them to be. As the boys began to feel less defensive in talking with us, they became more inclined to reveal what was really going on in their lives and more willing to discuss sensitive issues.

In retrospect, it is interesting to see how God was moving in our lives to prepare all of us for a parenting ministry. An integral part of this plan was meeting Lee Long at the facility. His experience as a Christian therapist working with troubled teens provided a unique and valuable perspective to what later became the *Parenting by Design* curriculum.

## LEE'S BOX

As I counseled kids and their families at the facility, I realized how often dysfunctional parenting styles were turning up in the family system. Rather than producing the results the parents sought, these parenting methods were having an opposite effect—they were exacerbating their kids' problems and were counterproductive to the therapeutic process. Puzzled that many kids of well-meaning parents were in our program, I thought about my family and the parenting example set by my father and grandfather. Although I greatly admired both men, I decided to do it differently with my kids. I vowed I would try not to yell at them, lose my temper and spank out of anger, or make my kids fear me when I'm wasn't happy with something they did. If I wanted a different experience for my kids, I knew I would have to be diligent to avoid repeating the patterns of my father and grandfather.

My work with the kids at the rehabilitation program also revealed an interesting truth. When I asked them what they thought God was like, most described a God that sounded a lot like their own father. If Dad was permissive, the child tended to see God as overly concerned that everyone was happy. These kids seemed to assume that God didn't care how much they sinned because He would always rescue them and make things right.

On the other hand, if Dad was a strict disciplinarian, the child saw God as impatient, judgmental, and quick to punish when they stepped out of line. These kids were scared of God and not very interested in a relationship with Him. To them, God seemed mean-spirited. I observed this tendency in my own life. Deep down in my heart, I carried an image of a lightning-bolt-throwing God who was ready to zap me every time I made a mistake. I'll admit it; I was a little afraid of God and prone to hide from Him at times.

About that time, God had a little surprise for my wife, Charlotte, and me—she was pregnant with our first child! But after the initial excitement, fear crept in. I was going to be responsible for a child. Realizing my daughter's image of God would be influenced by my example, I knew I would have to change the way I handled my anger, among other things. It was time to take an honest inventory of my life. This meant I needed to trust God with my fears, rather than trying to keep them from God and control them on my own. God was giving me this little baby, and He would have to equip me to raise her.

I believe my time in Colorado working with families saved my family. It shaped my relationship with my kids—I now have three—because I turned my family legacy of anger over to the Lord. It saved my relationship with my wife because she did not have to stand between my children and me and protect them from my anger. I learned that no parent is perfect and that I will fail at times, just as my father and grandfather did. But I also learned that my failures give me an opportunity to model humility for my kids.

This was beautifully demonstrated while I worked at the facility in Colorado. A short time after my daughter was born, I got a call from my father. We were in the middle of a conversation about what it meant to be a father and to be a godly example for our children, and I was sharing that I didn't want my daughter to have to endure the struggles I was seeing at the facility. And then—in a moment I will never forget—my father admitted the mistakes he had made while parenting me.

He had been thinking about the past and wanted to ask me to forgive him for his shortcomings. My dad said, "I hope you know that I love you. I hope you know that I was doing what I did out of love, although I know now I was wrong. Please forgive me for going about it the way I did." I will never forget how my father modeled humility for me in this most powerful way. I believe his humble act of confession showed me how to be a true father.

As we prepared for our first child, I did what a lot of expectant parents do: I read parenting books. Being a therapist at an adolescent treatment center scared me, and I didn't want my daughter to end up in a program like ours. As I read, however, I found a significant amount of the parenting advice was about "authority," "control," and "punishment." It seemed the writers were pitting the parents against the children. Something wasn't right. My experience was that a lot of kids had problems that were partially *caused* by this kind of parenting. I didn't want to become my new daughter's adversary. It seemed so unlike the way God parents us.

Sure enough, as I studied biblical parenting principles, I was pleased to learn that the Bible presents a very different paradigm. I discovered that our heavenly Father relies far more on His relationship *with* us than His authority *over* us. He teaches us through our experiences and consequences much more than He does by controlling our actions. He provides an example of holy living, but He doesn't force us to follow it. And He uses the consequences of our experiences to help us understand how to make better choices in the future. God's parenting style is not "My way or the highway." I ended up putting those parenting books in the trash and started studying how to parent my kids the way God has parented me.

While our son was in treatment in Colorado, we shared with friends in Fort Worth some of the parenting principles we were learning. To our surprise, we began to get phone calls from parents seeking advice about what to do with their kids. How ironic that we—the parents with a teenager in treatment—were being asked for advice!

During the parenting classes we attended at the facility that spring, Michelle remembers making a bargain with God. She said, "Lord, I think this is great information, and I really believe our friends in Fort Worth need to hear this. I don't think I can teach it to them, but if You give me the opportunity, I'm willing to help make a class happen." She remembers feeling pretty sure that God would not take her up on the bargain! But neither of us was prepared for the sequence of events that unfolded over the next few months.

Our son graduated from the treatment program in May 2004, returned home, and got ready to finish his senior year at a local public high school. About a month later, Lee called to tell us he was moving to the Dallas-Fort Worth area. And not long after that, Mark, another therapist who taught parenting classes at the facility, moved to the area.

About the same time, we learned about a brand-new ministry within our church called Soul Care. Greg, the pastor over Soul Care, was looking for unique ways to nurture and care for the congregation. God had handed us the opportunity on a silver platter. We got together with Greg, Lee, and Mark to discuss the logistics of our first parenting class.

By the fall of 2004, Mark and Lee were leading the first Parenting by Design class at our church in Fort Worth. Michelle and I handled the administrative duties. The curriculum was a combination of biblical principles, practical tools we had learned from existing curriculums, and many lessons from Lee and Mark's counseling experiences. The response to the initial class was so positive we followed it up with another class at the church. During the next year, we held several more classes in Fort Worth and began a series in Houston as well.

One of the most rewarding aspects of these classes was the mutual encouragement and support that emerged as parents became more comfortable revealing their fears and insecurities to the other class members. Bit by bit, it seemed as if they were willing to take off their "masks" and risk being authentic in order to become better parents. We found this interaction to be truly valuable for parents trying to implement the principles in real life because they had trustworthy others they could turn to when things got difficult. Getting a community of parents involved became a value of ours.

As 2006 rolled around, Michelle and I felt that we needed to get some formal training to counsel parents more effectively. We were both accepted into Dallas Theological Seminary's biblical counseling program that summer. In the meantime, Mark had taken another position that prevented him from teaching our classes anymore. Lee did not want to teach alone, so we racked our brains to come up with someone who could take over for Mark. When Lee suggested that Michelle and I should do it, we hesitated because we didn't feel equipped. But after much prayer and soul-searching, we decided to take on the challenge.

Our seminary training provided a wealth of new information that we incorporated into the curriculum. In fact, a class project became the basis for the daily parenting devotionals that are currently sent to people all over the world. In May 2010 Michelle graduated and became a Licensed Professional Counselor. She practices with Lee Long in Fort Worth. In December 2010 I graduated with a master's degree in Christian education. I also became executive pastor at Trinity Chapel Bible Church in Fort Worth.

And in just a few years, the small-group study in our church had grown into the ministry called Parenting by Design. We currently use many different means to reach parents, including our small-group series called "Principles and Practice," daily devotionals, newsletters, an interactive website (parentingbydesign.com), discussion groups, DVDs, audios, and social media.

As it turned out, the day we dropped off our son at the treatment facility was a huge day in his life, but it was also a dramatic turning point in ours. As we enrolled our son, we hoped he would be changed, but we found God had much bigger plans. He embraced us, encouraged us, and introduced us to Lee. In the midst of our struggles, we begged God for answers and wondered what we had done to deserve such punishment. And what we came to realize was that God wasn't punishing us. He was saving us. And He was leading us on the path toward Parenting by Design.

None of us planned for a ministry to grow out of our experience. But God had other plans, and we wouldn't have it any other way. We love the opportunities this ministry affords us to meet and counsel with other parents. We believe God is the perfect model of parenthood and that the parenting principles found throughout the Bible are just as applicable to today's families as they were when they were written. For those who are struggling, we offer the encouragement that God can redeem *anything*.

Of course, Michelle and I still make mistakes and our old tendencies creep back in at times, but we recognize them for what they are: imperfect responses from sinners in a fallen world. If you're looking for a book by people who have always done it right, this isn't the book for you. We have never been perfect. We struggled for many years. But we've learned what it is like to live as fallen parents with fallen kids in a fallen world. What we've learned has changed our family dramatically, and we hope you will find the truth in this book to help you change your family too.

There is one more thing you should know. We would love to guarantee that by following these principles your kids won't get into trouble, but we can't. We've known some of the greatest parents in the world, godly men and women, whose kids have strayed. Sometimes, kids are taught the right things, hear the right words, experience life in a loving, God-fearing home, and still choose to follow a different path. That is truly hard. We cannot give you a few easy steps that will ensure happy, healthy kids. We can, however, give you principles and practices that will greatly enhance your parenting efforts, build authentic relationships with your kids, and give your children the best chance for real, godly success in the world. It *is* possible to develop relationships with your kids that encourage them to come to you with serious issues and for you to walk alongside them as they face those issues. That may not guarantee a good result, but it makes it much more likely.

In the pages of this book, we will share these key parenting practices. We also want to assure you it's never too late, no matter how old your kids are. Our boys were sixteen and eighteen when Bob entered treatment. We discovered that any parent-child relationship could be transformed at any age. When we started to implement these principles, the ship began to turn around for our family. The turn was slow—big ships don't turn very quickly—but we began to see a difference in the way our family communicated. Our hope is that these principles will help you and will impact your home as much as they have impacted ours.

You should know the road is usually bumpy. Ours certainly was. Three and a half years after Bob graduated from the adolescent treatment program, we discovered the unthinkable: he had relapsed! He was living at home, going to college, and working at a local sandwich shop. We had every reason to think he was doing well after his first rehab experience, but the issues that caused his relapse became more severe than before. Having been involved in this parenting ministry for a couple of years, we knew a strong response was necessary. And because Bob had stolen money from us, we knew he would have to face more severe consequences for his poor choices. We told him how much we loved him, but we also gave him a tough choice: enter a second long-term treatment program or we would press charges and he would likely go to prison. On an intellectual level, the choices were clear, but emotionally, it was the most heart-wrenching thing we had done in our lives.

I'll admit that when this second big crisis erupted, I was very angry with my son and with God. I felt we had done everything we knew to do. We had changed our parenting style. We believed we were communicating well with both of our sons. Michelle and I had recommitted our spiritual lives. We were working in full-time ministry at Parenting by Design and going to seminary part-time. I felt God *owed* me relief from this problem. I screamed at God in my prayers, "How could You let this happen? I want my son back!"

Fortunately, Bob agreed to go to the treatment program. This program required a commitment of eighteen to twenty-four months. The participants were obligated to work as many as forty-eight hours per week at manual labor to pay their expenses. So, as you can imagine, staying in the program took a lot of effort. We were on pins and needles for the first few weeks because we knew our son could leave whenever he wanted. Thank God, he didn't because that would have left us with only one choice—to press charges—and we desperately didn't want it to come to that.

The amazing thing is that even this part of God's plan for our family turned out much better than we had dreamed. Of course, God had always known a second rehab was going to be necessary to heal and restore Bob. God also knew he would be transformed by the experience. And he was. There was little television, so he became a voracious reader. He began reading the Bible every day. He listened to Christian radio at work and became incredibly well versed in theology and Christian living. And as his Bible knowledge increased, so did his understanding of his condition. He began to understand he could never be free of his addictions without Christ. Other residents of the program were in the same spiritual condition, and they prayed for and helped each other. After just three months, he recommitted himself to Christ.

God opened the doors of Bob's treatment facility to Parenting by Design as well. We held two Parenting by Design classes and handed out more than fifty certificates of completion to residents. We hosted twice-a-month Bible studies and once-a-month worship services. Many of the residents became our friends. Those doors never would have opened without our son's issues.

We are not naïve. God gives no guarantees except that He will walk through our suffering with us. But Bob is a believer who has had a crash course on pain and suffering. He has an intimate understanding of addiction issues and wants to help others. He is now happily married, expecting his first child, and attending Bible college with the goal of being a pastor one day.

And we learned yet again that God truly can redeem anything. "We know that in all things God works for the good of those who love him, who have been called according to his purpose" (Rom. 8:28).

# CHAPTER 2

# RAISING "SUCCESSFUL" KIDS

How often are you in a group of parents, talking about your families, and the conversation turns into a subtle competition to see whose kids are the most "successful"? The parents of the athletes are bragging about last night's game. The parents of the dancer are talking about the special costumes they bought for the solos their daughter will perform at the next recital. The smart kids' parents are upset with the way the valedictorian was chosen. This can leave the parents of the kids who are not at the top of the heap racking their brains for something about their children they can add to the conversation.

You're not alone if you find yourself on the outside of these conversations. In fact, you are among the majority of parents whose kids will not be the top scorer, prima ballerina, or valedictorian. (I wish I could say the competition is less intense in Christian circles, but that is just not the case.) Our culture admires and celebrates the accomplishments of its so-called superstars, and we are led to believe that "stardom" is the ultimate achievement. When our kids fall short of that goal, as most of them will, we feel a sense of disappointment. So we find ourselves pushing our children to achieve *something!*

This is a tough subject to address, and we don't want to come across as harsh and condemning. We certainly have been there ourselves. But this reality is repeated day in and day out and our kids suffer because of it. Why? Because although God has gifted each one of our kids in unique and different ways, our tendency is to give an exaggerated amount of attention to high-profile gifts and skills, giving our children the impression that some talents are not as valuable as others. When we do this, we have fallen into the age-old trap of valuing gifts and skills using the world's definition of "success." If you want to see a biblical example of people falling into this trap, read 1 Corinthians 12:12–26.

## Uncovering Parenting Motivations

Only one perfect person has walked the earth, and we are not He. We'll learn a lot about God's parenting style in the following pages, but we have to realize we will all fall short of His standards (Rom. 3:23). As we encourage you to dig deeper into your motivations, you may realize how often your parenting decisions are actually meeting *your* needs rather than meeting your *kids'* needs. This can be difficult to recognize at first because you are usually not conscious of it, but your insecurities, desires, and fears have a profound effect on your parenting decisions. In addition, most parents have a deeply felt desire to raise "successful" children. This was certainly true in our family.

Of course, there is nothing wrong with trying to raise our kids for success; the problem lies in the way we define success. In the next few chapters, we will ask you to step back and take a look at the goals and desires you have for your children. Wading into these waters is never easy. Courage and strength are essential to honestly examine your motives, insecurities, and fears to see how they are affecting your parenting decisions. Take a moment to ask God to humbly prepare you to listen to His wisdom and direction before you start.

When Michelle and I embarked on this new path, we realized the degree to which our culture equates good parenting with outward results and how that had become deeply ingrained in us. We also discovered the many ways we had tried to meet our needs through our kids. Like us, many parents unconsciously use their children to validate themselves or to achieve some goal that eluded them when they were children. Together, we will try to break down our false ideas about success and replace them with God's goals and purposes. Our hope is that this book will encourage and excite you to give your children the tools and guidance they need to grow into the people God designed them to be.

## Parenting for "Success"

How do you know whether you're a "successful" parent? A lot of us have pretty good general answers to that question that measure success by the faith of our kids, their love for God and others, their happiness and health, and so on. But while we have a broad idea of what success looks like to us, we begin to run into problems when we examine whether we are actually parenting our kids toward those goals. Our agenda for our kids often goes further than the broad ideals we profess. This underlying, unstated agenda can move us unconsciously from parenting for God's glory to parenting for the world's approval.

In his book *Raising Kids for True Greatness*,[1] Tim Kimmel talks about a principle he calls the "success trap." His theory is that while our overarching goals for parenting may be godly ones, we often fail to see how our daily decisions reveal worldly subgoals. The fact is we are easily deceived by our culture's view of success, and the world's influence is often far more pervasive than we imagine. In fact, despite our expressed intention, many of us are inadvertently parenting our kids toward the world's definition of success.

We will share an example. All of us know kids are required to go to school, but many parents get tied up in knots about which school is best. Of course, the choice of a school is very important and we know every school is not alike. And while you may want your kids to attend the best possible school for their particular gifts, some of the lengths we go to see that our kids get the best education can be almost comical. Even at the preschool level, the competition among parents can be intense!

## MICHELLE'S BOX

I remember when a Christian friend called to tell me she was pregnant. But her joy took a somber turn when she called me in a panic a few weeks later. She was certain she had missed the deadline to sign up her *unborn* child for the city's most prestigious preschool ... a school he or she wouldn't even attend until age three! Apparently, this preschool had a reputation for producing "high achievers." Many parents believed this preschool led directly to their children being accepted into great colleges. Entrance into the preschool became so competitive that if a mother-to-be wanted to reserve a spot, she had to sign up as soon as she found out she was pregnant! If she waited, all the spots would be filled before the babies were even born. But that wasn't all. At age two and a half, the child had to go through an admissions process. Acceptance ultimately depended on the school's director. Desperate parents showered the director of the preschool with all types of gifts to enhance the odds of their child being accepted. In their efforts to ensure success for their kids, the parents had seriously overblown the importance of this little preschool. My friend is not superficial, but even she got swept up in the cultural tide of her peer group who convinced her that this preschool was an essential part of being a "good" parent.

Of course, most parents want their children to have the best education possible. That's not wrong, but you have to ask why you want to enroll your kids in a particular school. It may be because that school is best suited to develop their gifts, passions, and skills. But if you are honest, some of the reasons you choose a school may also be from a desire for status, glory, or worldly success. A prestigious school is not ideal for every child, and it can be very difficult to discern between the desires of our culture and the desires of God. We may encounter pressure from friends and family to follow the path to "success" and find ourselves rationalizing our decisions. But God calls us to resist these pressures, and He promises to stand with us when we do. (See 1 Peter 5:9.)

I had to think long and hard about Bob's decision to go to the local public high school when he got out of his first rehab. He could have chosen to go back to the excellent private school he had attended since kindergarten. Academically, it was superior to the public school. But along with its highly pedigreed environment came some unique social and financial opportunities and pressures. I had seen this as an advantage in the past, but now I had to examine my motivations for wanting to send him back there. Was that truly the best place for him? The decision was difficult, but in the end, I had to trust God and pray for peace. We let Bob make the choice, and he decided to finish up at the public school.

Our educational goals are also greatly influenced by the kind of job we'd like for our kids. We want them to have a good education so they can get a good job and have a successful career. There's nothing wrong with that, right? But here's the question: how will we define a successful career?

Often, our desire is for our kids to make enough money to buy the things they need and want. Consequently, our idea of a good job is largely defined by the amount of money it pays. We rationalize by saying we want our kids to "have a better life" than we had, and we fail to see the irony in pursuing more *money* as the route to a so-called "better life." Rather than looking at the workplace as a place where they can use their gifts to honor God, we see it as a way for our kids to make enough money to achieve a certain type of lifestyle. I've had more than one friend admit how difficult it was when their son or daughter chose a career in ministry because they knew it wouldn't provide the standard of living they wanted their kids to have.

In addition to the money, we look at the opportunity for promotions and of moving up the corporate ladder as part of our concept of a good career. Promotions generally mean greater independence and more authority over others. Our goal for this upward advancement may be for our kids to be in a better position to exert a godly influence in their workplace and culture, but there's also the distinct possibility that we want our kids to hold positions of increasing power so they can be the ones *exercising* authority rather than being *subject* to it. Can you see how quickly and surreptitiously *worthy* goals are converted into well-disguised *worldly* goals?

Another area where cultural pressure has an influence is in your kids' appearance. A lot of money is spent by advertisers to convince us we need to have the right clothes, jewelry, and cosmetics. "Clothes make the man," right? Everybody wants to look like they belong, and older kids are especially aware when their appearance doesn't reflect the identity they want to cultivate.

But appearances are deceiving. Many of us hide our insecurities behind our outward appearance, and we spend billions of dollars to do it. Some people will even risk their health. High school girls have plastic surgery to make them look sexier. Boys are working out and taking steroids to bulk up and look "good." The role models for our kids are actors, actresses, and athletes who are impossibly good looking. The media tell us that beauty is the ticket to attracting the opposite sex, and romances among the young and beautiful are portrayed as sure signs of significance and success.

Besides the messages they receive from the media, our kids watch us as well. Our actions speak louder than words. We send a confusing message when we profess godly values but spend much of our time, money, and efforts on our appearances. What our kids internalize is that despite what we say, it really is important to look as beautiful as possible. We need to consider what our actions communicate about where we derive our sense of worth.

Consider this passage describing Christ: "He had no beauty or majesty to attract us to him, nothing in his appearance that we should desire him" (Isa. 53:2). Clearly, an attractive appearance was not one of God's priorities.

In addition to money, power, and beauty, another desire many parents have for their kids is recognition. Our culture unashamedly endorses the pursuit of fame. Go to any Little League ballpark and listen as parents scream "helpful" instructions to their kids. Go to a pine-box derby and stare in wonder at the carefully crafted cars, with full aerodynamic features and graphite-slicked axles that the "kids" allegedly made. And don't think Christian parents are exempt from fame's lure. I cringed when I heard about the antics of a couple that regularly attend our church and are very active in small groups. Apparently, every time they go to a high school football game to watch their son, a transformation occurs. They scream at the referees, players, and coaches on the other team. They have been known to direct tirades at players on their son's team when they make a bad play. More than once, they have been asked by the officials to leave the stadium. And their son attends a private Christian school! This irony is not lost on nonbelievers and is often the topic of Monday morning discussions.

Perhaps you have noticed parents encouraging their children to chase awards and hold offices in school organizations in order to build a better college resume. That sounds like an admirable pursuit, but while it might enhance their odds for admission, what are we sacrificing in the process? Aren't we teaching our children that it is okay to pursue positions of leadership for self-serving purposes? Instead, shouldn't we encourage them to be leaders because they have a genuine interest in an organization and the service it provides?

Recognition in and of itself isn't wrong, but we have to ask ourselves if we seek it for our glory or God's. If we're serving God in response to the priceless gift He gives us, we shouldn't care about receiving worldly recognition. But when we crave it for ourselves and our kids, we set both of us up for disappointment. Fame fades quickly and never satisfies for long.

No doubt about it, we live in a world that values money, power, beauty, and fame. This message is pounded into our brains from the minute we wake up until our heads touch the pillow. The lure is difficult to resist and you will be given lots of opportunities to compromise. Ask God for the wisdom and strength to break free from the culture's siren call. Use His worldview as the grid through which you evaluate the temptations that are thrown in your path. With His glory as your ultimate goal, you can unmask the culture's goals and keep pursuing God's.

## LEE'S BOX

In my office, I see many adolescents who get mixed messages from their parents. These kids tell me their parents claim to care about God's goals and the lessons the Bible teaches but seem more concerned about their kids' popularity, proper appearance, achievements in athletics or academics, or for them to be part of the right groups and activities. I am amazed by how quickly kids pick up on what their parents truly value. One of the biggest challenges for me is helping parents see the *real* messages they send their kids.

I also have seen the relational healing that takes place when parents admit their mistakes. One teenage boy was angry with his parents for pressuring him to live up to standards he saw as superficial and shallow. He described them as hypocrites and acted out in rebellion. When his parents had a dramatic change of heart and their value system changed, he recognized it immediately. Because they honestly examined their lives, his anger subsided and he was able to look at his own life.

How does God define success? Consider what Jesus says in Matthew 20:26–28. "Whoever wants to become great among you must be your servant, and whoever wants to be first must be your slave—just as the Son of Man did not come to be served, but to serve, and to give his life as a ransom for many."

God puts up His Son as the model for our kids. Paul says a similar thing in Philippians 2:3–5. "Do nothing out of selfish ambition or vain conceit, but in humility consider others better than yourselves. Each of you should look not only to your own interests, but also to the interests of others. Your attitude should be the same as that of Christ Jesus."

You may not have thought about imitating Christ as the ideal for your kids, but that's how God defines success. If our children serve God and other people unselfishly, putting others first, they will be a huge success in God's eyes.

For God, life isn't about money, power, beauty, and fame. Michelle and I came to this realization late in life and decided we would try to parent our boys to succeed on God's terms, not the world's. Great goal, but hard to implement. Even now, we are constantly amazed at how much influence the world has on our thoughts and actions. A sure sign of this influence is when we need our kids to excel so others will see us as successful parents. Seeking validation by the world's values or by other people's perceptions will never satisfy, because those things are fickle and illusory, and that isn't how God validates us as fathers and mothers.

We like the way Kimmel expresses God's definition of success. "A passionate love for God that demonstrates itself in an unquenchable love and concern for others."[2] If those words describe your child as he or she grows up—regardless of the accumulation of money, power, beauty, and fame—could you live with that? That's a big change for most of us, but it's essential if we're to guide our children to be the people God created them to be.

Don't underestimate how difficult it is to avoid the success trap. You'll find yourselves in conversations with other parents, and inevitably, the discussions will reflect a preoccupation with money, power, beauty, and fame. It takes a deliberate effort to put aside the standards of other parents and stick with God's values. You will find it difficult to keep from gravitating toward the world's values in your own thinking—to allow your children to cause a little embarrassment at times or to fall short of other people's ideals. But with God's help, you can do it. You can focus on the things that will promote genuine spiritual growth in their lives. Thankfully, God promises to equip you if you ask. (See James 1:5.)

Remember God is more interested in your children than you are. He has a plan for each and every life. He created our children and us with a purpose in mind, and He knows every detail of our lives. (See Ps. 139:1–4.) That's why we named our ministry Parenting by Design. It is our mission to help parents discover God's design for children and to help them live out that design. You can be certain that if God has a purpose for the lives of your family, He will be there to help you discover it and equip you to carry it out.

## Bringing It Home

I have been convicted by the idea of the success trap. It is prevalent in the lives of every group of people, whether you live in affluence in America or poverty in Liberia. Each time I recognize it, I am reminded of how often I think about those four concepts—money, power, beauty, and fame—and how willing I am to compromise to get them. Our hope is that you will recognize those false markers of success when you see them. That is the first step toward changing your mind-set. This will not be easy, because it is a big part of our culture. A lot of powerful forces line up against God's perspective on success, including the advertising industry, the media, Hollywood, and other parents. But God will have the final say, and when I stand before Him, I long to hear Him say, "Well done."

# CHAPTER 3

# WHAT IS YOUR PARENTING STYLE?

Sherry grew up with strict, disciplinarian parents. They didn't allow her to question the rules they set and they expected immediate obedience. If she suggested alternatives or offered a different point of view, her parents often responded with anger or punishment. Even though they provided for all her material needs, they could be cold and intimidating at times. The threat of punishment and fear of rejection kept her in line, but it came at a cost. Because Sherry desperately craved her parents' attention and approval, she believed these things were performance based. As a result, she made a determined effort to prove her worth not only to her parents but also to other adults in her life. And in this respect, she was "successful." Her efforts won her many honors and awards. On the outside, she looked like an overachiever, but on the inside, she was anxious and insecure. When she had her own children, Sherry was determined to make them feel good about themselves so they would never doubt her love.

Jason was raised in a home with a loving but micromanaging mom. She had an opinion about almost every aspect of his life. If he had a school project, she would give him lots of suggestions and often ended up doing much of the project herself. Jason knew she loved him, but he grew up feeling confined and stifled. He vowed that when he had kids, he would be a more relaxed parent. He wouldn't breathe down their necks and supervise every decision. He wanted to give them the freedom to do things their own way.

Like it or not, our parenting style is heavily influenced by the style of our parents. If we were pleased with the way we were raised, we'll try to raise our kids the same way. But if we were disappointed in our parents, we may try an opposite approach. Like Sherry and Jason, we may adopt a different parenting style in order to avoid making the same mistakes. Sometimes, this causes us to overcompensate by leaning too far in the other parenting direction. For example, if our parents were harsh or disconnected, we may become an overly doting parent. If we were overprotected, we may have a tendency to be too permissive.

Of course, we may repeat the same dysfunctional patterns passed down from our parents. If our parents had a tendency to withdraw when angry, we may reenact this pattern with our children by giving them the silent treatment or playing the "martyr." If our parents were overly involved and enmeshed in our lives, we may repeat this relational pattern and have difficulty letting our kids have some freedom. An important first step to developing an effective parenting style is being willing to look at experiences from our childhood and consider how they may be influencing our parenting practices today.

## LEE'S BOX

I often see parents trying to undo what happened to them as children. For instance, if they didn't get much attention as children, they compensate by being overly involved in the lives of their children. If they wish their parents had pushed them in sports or academics, they tend to push their kids in these areas. If they weren't popular, they go out of their way to make sure their kids have plenty of opportunities to socialize with the "cool" group.

No one wants their children to repeat painful childhood experiences, but we must remember that our children are not growing up in the same family situation we grew up in. They have different parents, different gifts, and different circumstances. This was true of thirteen-year-old Monica. When Monica was born, her mother was a single mom who had dropped out of high school to take care of her.

Monica's mother deeply regretted not graduating from high school, and she didn't want her daughter to follow in her footsteps. To give Monica the best education possible, she enrolled her in many special academic programs. The only problem was that Monica wasn't that interested in the subjects of these programs. Monica knew the fear and regret that motivated her mother, and she resented being forced into her mother's mold for "success." In the counseling office, Monica said, "I understand why my mom is making me do this stuff—she's afraid I'm going to make the same mistakes she made. But I'm not her. I wish she trusted me enough to give me the chance to sign up for activities *I'm* interested in."

Like this mother, we create new problems when we parent to undo our pain. We miss seeing our kids as the unique people God created them to be and fail to allow their experiences to be a reflection of their own journey.

One of the most familiar parenting verses in the Bible is Proverbs 22:6, which says, "Train a child in the way he should go, and when he is old he will not turn from it." Many books and sermons on parenting quote this verse. In reading through the material, we've noticed that the emphasis tends to be on one just one aspect: the training. The teaching seems to suggest that "training" your children is accomplished by giving instructions and correction and demanding unswerving and immediate compliance and obedience. A number of popular parenting curricula teach this method, sometimes labeled "first-time obedience." But before we jump in and start "training" our kids, let's pause and take a careful look at Proverbs 22:6.

### The Way He Should Go

What exactly is meant by the phrase "the way he should go"? For starters, we can be sure that "the way he should go" includes pointing our kids to God's framework for holy living, but another important aspect of this proverb often gets overlooked. The word translated "way" in the proverb is the Hebrew word *derek,* which can mean "way" or "road." It can also mean "characteristic manner." (See Prov. 30:18–19 for an example.) It seems obvious that the question we should ask *before* we start training is "What is the child's characteristic manner?" The truth is God has given each of us—including our kids—unique abilities and talents. He has designed us in a particular way for particular tasks that He has for us (Eph. 2:10). It is important to remember that when God says "the way he should go," He's talking about *His* design for the child, not *ours*. This should encourage us to be students of our children. How do they relate to others? What are their natural talents? How do they see the world? What is their temperament? We should be discovering and nurturing our children's God-given gifts and abilities instead of pushing them to develop the gifts we'd prefer for them to have. In this way, we help them fulfill God's purpose for their lives.

I found this out the hard way. I remember noticing when our oldest son, Ben, was about three years old that he was left-handed. That was pretty exciting for a dad who loves baseball. I started to imagine him playing first base, where lefties are always in demand, and maybe even pitching. I had big dreams for my little lefty.

I coached Little League for six or seven years and tried my best to hone Ben's baseball skills. But the more I worked at it, the more frustrated we both became. I probably should have realized he didn't have any desire to learn to play baseball. He didn't even like it. But I was determined. At one point, I offered to pay him a dollar for every time he *swung* at the ball! Eventually, I had to let go of my desire and stop trying to force him to conform to my design for his life. My plan wasn't God's plan, and trying to make Ben a baseball player was never going to work.

The truth was Ben had always been a talented artist. From his earliest years, when he wanted to tell you a story, he would draw it out. He spent hours as a child drawing intricate pictures. During his senior year in high school, he became even more focused on his painting. Voilà! We discovered what he had probably always felt in his heart—he was an artist, not a baseball player. Set free to pursue God's design for his life, he eventually transferred to Boston University's fine arts program. He graduated, and at the time of the release of this book, he is pursuing a career as an artist. And you know what? I love to talk with Ben about painting. His passion is contagious and exciting. He's a *painter!* If I had figured that out years ago, it would have saved both of us a lot of frustration.

We need to stop holding on so tightly to our designs for our kids. Children eventually leave home, and our job as parents is to help them get ready. They become more independent each day, and that's a healthy process that we can either assist or resist. When we help them discover how God designed and gifted them, we can help them grow according to that design. In the process, they become happier and more confident in their gifts and abilities. And we can encourage them to become more dependent on God as they become less dependent on us.

## Bonding, Boundaries, and Balance

One of our goals for this book is to suggest a biblical model for balanced parenting. But first we need to understand how we get out of balance—why our parenting pendulum wants to swing toward the extremes. To do that, we'll look at the tension between bonding and boundaries and how it plays out in three different styles of parenting.

Bonding is the process of learning to be close to another person. Boundaries are what make us distinct from other people. We need both in any relationship. We can get so bonded to someone that we lose our identity in theirs, but we can also erect so many boundaries that we are unable to have close, meaningful relationships. A balance between bonding and boundaries is necessary to function well in a relationship, but it's also easy to get out of balance, especially with our kids. When that happens—when we lean too far toward either bonding or boundaries—we may become either a rescuer or a dictator. These terms describe off-balance parents.

The balanced parent adopts the counselor parenting style—the style that corresponds to the balanced parenting style of our heavenly Father. Though most of you will exhibit characteristics of all three styles, you will probably find yourself gravitating toward one style in particular. So let's look at the characteristics of each and consider how kids tend to react to each style of parenting.

## The Rescuer

When rescuers lose their relational "balance," it is almost always toward the bonding side. They generally have trouble establishing boundaries and following through with appropriate consequences. Rescuers are anxious when their children make painful mistakes, so they hover, protect, and try to rescue their kids from pain. They are motivated by love, of course; most rescuers will tell you that their *job* is to protect their children from pain. That is one of the ways they feel they can express their love for their kids.

The rescuer rarely considers whether rescuing a child from pain really is the most loving thing they can do. The fact is that most kids have a desire to be competent and to solve problems. When they are successful in those situations, they gain confidence and become more prepared for life on their own. Rescuers don't understand that the sacrifices they make in the name of love may actually send their kids the negative implied message that says, "You're weak and fragile, and you need me to rescue you." These parents don't mean to imply that their children are actually weak or fragile, but that is the unspoken message the kids receive.

We believe the most loving thing parents can do is to allow their children to solve age-appropriate problems while they walk alongside them empathetically. When they let their children try to solve problems, parents are letting their kids know that they believe in their capabilities and that mistakes are not the end of the world.

But let's be honest: the act of rescuing has a seductive appeal. For parents who sometimes feel unimportant, unappreciated, or neglected, rescuing their kids can make them feel needed. Unfortunately, this habit of fostering dependence usually backfires. The message "I love you so much I would do anything for you" often comes with an expectation that the child will be appreciative. But kids who are constantly rescued begin to feel entitled instead. Because they have been rescued many times, when a difficult or painful situation comes along, they expect the rescuer to get them out of it. They can even get angry when the parent doesn't ride to the rescue.

We saw an example of this with a teenager who went off to college. During the semester, he scheduled a trip to see a friend at another school. He made his reservations with the airline and took care of all the arrangements. His mom, anxious to make sure everything had gone all right, called him after he was supposed to have landed and asked him how the flight went. "Oh, I missed the plane," he said.

"Really! What happened?" she asked.

"You're not going to believe it. No one from the airline called to remind me about the flight!" he exclaimed.

His parents had rescued him so often he expected it from everyone. They hadn't prepared him for how the world really works. Many parents seem to think that when their kids turn eighteen, they will automatically become responsible and mature. They keep rescuing their kids until they move away from home, failing to consider that they may be postponing important learning opportunities.

The rescuing process typically starts early. In cars at school around lunchtime, have you seen the line of parents bringing forgotten lunches, uniforms, equipment, or homework? If you have, you've probably also seen the kids waiting impatiently, wondering why Mom or Dad didn't get there faster! Entitlement is almost always the result of repeated rescues.

Proverbs 19:19 has a good take on rescuing. "A hot-tempered man must pay the penalty; if you rescue him, you will have to do it again." Our kids need to face the consequences of their choices. They need to understand the biblical concepts of sowing and reaping. If they don't learn to face consequences early in life, they will end up facing them later when the stakes are higher and the rescuer isn't there to save them. When a chronically rescued kid finds himself on his own, don't be surprised if he begins looking for someone else to rescue him. Sadly, many people with less than pure motives are willing to take on that role. Isn't it much better to allow your kids to struggle with some trials while you can walk with them and prepare them to face challenges on their own?

## The Dictator

The opposite of the rescuer is the dictator. This is a parent who is so focused on maintaining boundaries that bonding becomes secondary. Like rescuers, dictators don't want their kids to make mistakes, but for entirely different reasons. Avoiding pain isn't their primary issue; instead, they are more focused on maintaining tight control of their kids, hoping to prevent mistakes.

Dictators believe the best way to control their children is by lecturing, issuing commands, and giving specific directions. While they establish clear expectations about acceptable behavior and the consequences for violating their rules, they usually do not give reasons or explanations for the rules they set. They expect children to obey without questioning. In the process, dictators send their kids a implied message that says, "You're incapable or incompetent, and you need me to tell you how to do things."

The dictator's obedience-oriented focus causes them to neglect the bonding side of parenting. In more extreme cases, kids can begin to fear the loss of the dictator's love if they don't obey quickly and completely.[3] This fear of rejection is usually a result of the dictator's delivery of discipline. When discipline is delivered without empathy, a child may see his parents' love as conditional—*obey or else!* While children of dictators are often obedient and high achieving, studies show they are also anxious and insecure.[4] Fearing the loss of love as a result of disobedience puts a child in a precarious position. He may end up afraid to take any risks, to question anyone in authority, or to take the lead in any endeavor—the classic withdrawal situation. Or he may get angry and rebel against the dictator—the classic case of rebellion. Dictators often push their kids into thinking they only have two options: fight or flight.

Proverbs 12:18 captures this relationship dynamic well: "Reckless words pierce like a sword, but the tongue of the wise brings healing." Dictatorial commands often contain reckless words and an implied message that pierces like a sword. "You can't do it" is a harsh thing for a kid to hear. A dictatorial style can convince kids they can't measure up.

Another drawback to the dictator's approach is that it limits the growth of the child's intellectual abilities. When children are not given reasons to help them understand the rules or encouraged to express their thoughts and feelings, their language and reasoning skills can be stunted. Need proof? Children of parents who are dictators score lower on verbal tests of intelligence than children who are allowed to interact with their parents about rules and directives.[5]

## The Counselor

Where's the middle ground between bonding and boundaries? What does balance between a rescuer and a dictator look like? We use the term *counselor* to describe a parent who walks between the two extremes effectively. In the therapeutic setting, a counselor's job is to help a client gain insight into his situation and find the inner strength to develop a healthier lifestyle. This requires a lot of listening and open-ended questioning on the counselor's part to discover what's going on. The counselor must ask questions to find out whether he understands the client's issues correctly or whether he needs more information. A client will feel more secure and safe talking with a good counselor because he can tell from the questions that the counselor is truly interested in knowing him and helping him find the truth. Effective counselors allow their clients to come up with conclusions, although the counselor may be guiding them in that direction all along. That way, the client is more invested in pursuing potential solutions.

We recognize there are limits to this analogy. Parents can't say good-bye after an hour session and wait a week to see how things went. And unlike a professional counselor, parents have to implement consequences when their children make poor decisions. But we encourage parents to adopt the curiosity of a therapist when talking with their children, to establish a healthy and safe environment for their child to look inside and grow in understanding, and to give the child room to come up with and implement their own solutions.

Let's look at some Bible verses that encourage the balanced approach of the counselor's parenting style. "A man of knowledge uses words with restraint, and a man of understanding is even-tempered" (Prov. 17:27). The emphasis is on restraint, understanding, and an even temperament. How often do dictator parents violate these principles with angry or sarcastic words? Paul applies this principle specifically to parenting. "Fathers, do not exasperate your children; instead, bring them up in the training and instruction of the Lord" (Eph. 6:4). And in a related verse, he writes, "Fathers, do not embitter your children, or they will become discouraged" (Col. 3:21). These verses teach us that being harsh with our kids will discourage them and make it difficult for them to learn. Let's make it a point to encourage our kids instead to be known for being empathetic rather than for being angry and critical.

This will be much easier when we learn not to be so fearful of our children's mistakes. Unlike the rescuer or dictator, counselors understand that the mistakes children make are opportunities for them to grow rather than a reason for the parent to think he or she has failed. The apostle Paul describes this concept as *rejoicing* in struggles. "Not only so, but we also rejoice in our sufferings, because we know that suffering produces perseverance; perseverance, character; and character, hope" (Rom. 5:3–4). Most mistakes can be learning experiences that help kids become resourceful, self-confident decision makers and problem solvers. When we view mistakes this way, we don't have to protect our kids from everything they might do wrong. We have the privilege of being there to assist their growth as they navigate these challenges of life.

What does it look like to be the kind of parents who can counsel their children as they go through a trial? Balanced parents are warm, affectionate, and bonded with their kids, yet they respect the individuality of each child. They set appropriate boundaries for their kids and for themselves and consistently enforce rules, but they also give reasons and explanations for the rules. While they are firm in their discipline, they take time to listen to the child's point of view and allow him to explain his side of a situation, so long as he can do it in a respectful manner. Surprisingly, researchers have found that only about 10 to 12 percent of parents provide this balanced type of parenting.[6]

Most parents find it difficult to be both firm and loving, but it produces the most well-adjusted children. Following the children of balanced parents through longitudinal studies, researchers tell us these kids are more independent, are more self-controlled, are successful in relationships, and have a more positive outlook on life.[7]

In addition, balanced parents express confidence in their kids' ability to tackle problems and to grow from them. They assure their children they will walk with them through whatever issues they may face. That's being respectful of the way children should go—being an authority in their lives without dictating and being encouraging without rescuing. While counselor parents set age-appropriate boundaries and deliver effective consequences, they do it with an unconditional love that says, "I will never leave or forsake you no matter what mistakes you may make, and I am confident you will learn important lessons from the consequences. I am here for you, and I believe that you can learn how to handle the trials and the victories of life."

That's how God does it. He is the perfectly balanced parent. He loves us unconditionally, even in the face of our open rebellion, and He never compromises the truth to do it. He feels sorrow with us over the consequences we experience, pours out His compassion when we need it, and encourages us to learn valuable lessons and grow from our experiences. That's the kind of parents we should strive to be.

You know what's comforting to me? Even the perfect parent's children disobey—every one of them. God is perfect as a parent, yet all His children have fallen badly. That tells me the decisions my kids make aren't the sole determinant of whether I am a good or bad parent. We can't be too hard on ourselves. There was a time after my son had gone off to his first rehab when I didn't know what to say when people asked where he had gone. I felt that his being in a treatment program meant I was a failure as a father, so I would say he was "in boarding school" or something like that. But as time has gone on, I've realized that Bob's two treatment experiences were the most spiritually significant events in his life. Treatment programs gave him the time and the inclination to seek God and walk with Christ. It wasn't pleasant and I didn't like it—for his sake or mine. But that's what he needed, and God was good enough to give it to him. God wasn't punishing our family; He was saving us. The resulting relationship with our kids and our opportunity to minister to other parents is evidence He was providing for us all along. Our failure has become a success in His eyes and an example that we can rejoice in anticipation of what God will do with our suffering.

## The Perfect Example

One of the best examples of God's parenting style can be found in the story of the garden of Eden. We're used to reading it as the story of our origin and how sin entered the world, but when we look at it through the lens of parenting, it's very instructive. It's a great overview of how the perfect parent deals with His children, even in the face of blatant rebellion. Let's break it down.

From the very beginning, the authority structure in the garden was obvious. God as Creator was clearly in the position of authority over Adam. He set boundaries and established responsibilities. But even though God was Adam's authority, He wanted to be bonded with Adam as well. In the cool of the day, God walked and talked with Adam. He got down on Adam's level and enjoyed a personal relationship with him.

The Bible says God brought all the animals before Adam to see what he would name them (Gen. 2:19). This was a big honor because the act of naming something in ancient cultures was the same as being given authority over it. I imagine that life before the fall was a time when Adam felt safe and free enough that he could tell God anything without fear of judgment or condemnation.

Although God clearly had the power to force Adam to do *anything*, He didn't use that power. He allowed Adam to work the garden, to name the animals, and to care for all of God's creation as he saw fit. Each day must have been an adventure for Adam, having many choices of what to do and what to eat.

Although God gave Adam lots of choices, He set limits as well. There was one tree from which he was not allowed to eat. God laid out the consequence for a bad choice in that respect by saying, "When you eat of it, you shall surely die" (Gen. 2:17).

I find the next part of the story interesting. Although God established a clear boundary, He didn't micromanage Adam or force him to be obedient. If it had been me, I would have put that tree on the far side of the garden, five hundred feet in the air and surrounded by heavily armed angels. Every time Adam got close to it, I would have reminded him it was off limits, yelled at him to get away, or just moved it where he couldn't reach it. But not God. He established the boundary and the consequences, and He was willing to allow a bad choice to be made. There would be severe consequences, but God would use those consequences to further His plan for the human race.

Adam and Eve made what was probably the worst choice in history. They blatantly rebelled and ate from the forbidden tree. When they did, they found themselves feeling emotions they had never felt before: fear, shame, and guilt. What is instructive is how God responded to their rebellion. Instead of exploding in righteous anger, God was calm and began asking them questions. Adam and Eve were hiding because they knew they had done something wrong.

Before delivering the consequence, God asked them, "Where are you?" Obviously, He hadn't lost track of Adam and Eve; He knew exactly where they were. So why did He ask? He was asking for *their* sake, not for His. God knew the answer, but He knew He must help His children develop insight into their motivations. When God asked Adam where he was, Adam had to think about the fact that he was behind a tree and that he was "hiding." So far as we know, he had never hidden from God before; now God was asking him about it. I imagine Adam had to go through the whole scenario again in his mind before he could answer. He said he was naked and "afraid." Why? His response had to prompt a lot of soul-searching. And that was just the first question. God continued, "Who told you that you were naked?" "Have you eaten from the tree?" "What is this you have done?"

With every question and answer, Adam and Eve had to think about and own up to what they had done. They had to acknowledge that their bad choices had caused tremendous harm and a severe consequence was due. This is where God's example is even more daunting. He had established the consequence for crossing the boundary and it was time to keep His word. Adam and Eve would have to *die* for their transgression, not immediately but eventually. And they could no longer live in the perfect environment of the garden. I can't imagine what it was like to have to deliver a consequence like that. God could have avoided the dilemma by allowing Adam and Eve a do-over or by wiping them out and starting over with another couple. He chose neither option. Instead, He delivered the consequence that He promised. He was true to His word, thereby establishing that His word was trustworthy.

In delivering the consequence, God gives us one more example of His perfect parenthood. He delivered the consequence, but He did it in an incredibly empathetic way. Rather than throwing them out of the garden in anger and letting them stew about their new reality, He walked them out and explained how their lives would be different. He recognized the shame they felt because of their nakedness, so He fashioned clothes out of animal skins to cover their shame. He made it clear that although life would get tougher, He still loved them and would provide the ultimate solution to their predicament. (See Gen. 3:15.) And He gave them another chance to obey—to go out, to multiply, to subdue the earth, and to love Him.

What a wonderful blueprint for parenting. As parents in the image of God, we can assume the authority God gives us, yet also take the time to establish and enjoy a relationship with our kids. We can give our kids clear boundaries, allow them to make lots of choices within those boundaries, and be a part of the process with them. When our kids make a bad choice, we can let them know we love them yet empathetically deliver consequences that will teach them to make better choices in the future. We can cover our kids' shame by forgiving them and then change their environment to make compliance easier and give them another chance. We can remain a calm, strong presence in our kids' lives, never leaving or forsaking them. That's what parenting is all about.

## Bringing It Home

We'll explore these concepts more thoroughly later in this book, but you've probably seen yourself in one of the parenting styles we've covered so far. Maybe you recognize yourself as a rescuer or dictator. You've probably already noted which patterns will be most difficult to break. If you're a dictator, you may struggle giving your kids more choices; if you're a rescuer, you'll probably have a hard time watching your children suffer consequences. We all have different issues, but we're in the same boat. We're flawed parents trying to be balanced and to train our kids in a way that sets them up for success in God's eyes. God offers grace for parents who are trying to raise kids His way.

We hope this encourages you. Wherever you are in the parenting process, it's not too late to make some changes. For me, it has been a matter of letting go of my need to control and trying to shape our kids according to my designs. For Michelle, the turning point was realizing that struggles are necessary for our kids to grow and mature. For Lee, it was giving more choices and letting his kids have the freedom to fail without being upset or angry. Thankfully, God has been patient with us as we have sought to discover His purposes and plans for our families.

One more thing. As we've struggled and grown as parents, we have discovered that we aren't just parents; we're also children of our heavenly Father. We are as rebellious with Him as our kids will ever be with us. It is inspiring, frustrating, and educational all at the same time to look at our relationship with our heavenly Father and begin to understand what it is like to be a great parent. How does God put up with us? Why does He continue to love us, walk with us, and help us grow when we blatantly rebel against Him? He never leaves us. He has been with us all along, never stepping out of character or losing His composure.

When we see God as our true Father and ourselves as His children, we have a perfect parenting model. We see how He responds to us with infinite patience, kindness, and love. We see how He sticks by us even when we've done things we aren't proud of. His words in Hebrews 13:5—"I will never leave you or forsake you"—have proven true.

How can we learn to emulate Him? We can start by talking with Him. He's waiting. He's available day or night. We cannot stress the value of prayer enough. And we know that if we ask Him, He will help us discover the insight we need to raise our children. We can also learn about God's parenting style by studying the Bible. He is speaking to us right now, by the Holy Spirit, in the words of Scripture. I am always amazed when I read something in a morning devotional that applies directly to a current problem I have. Spend some time with your Father daily and turn your parenting issues over to Him. He is excited to help you!

# CHAPTER 4

# THE THREE E'S OF PARENTING

As our family sat around the dinner table and discussed the day, Michelle and I were pleased with how clearly we expressed ourselves. We pointed out where our boys had made mistakes, we let them know what they should do to avoid those mistakes in the future, and we assured them that if they followed our advice, they would be very grateful one day. All in all, we covered the bases thoroughly.

Surprisingly, neither of the boys said, "Mom and Dad, that was an awesome lecture. We've learned so much, and we'll never make those mistakes again. Thank you." In fact, in all our years of lecturing and nagging, we never once got that response. Instead, we got the opposite—a heated argument or glazed-over eyes, mumbled answers, and the feeling that what we'd said had gone in one ear and out the other. Why? Because lectures are not how most kids learn. While it is important to communicate your expectations to your kids, that doesn't always mean they will recognize your wisdom and make responsible choices. Too many parents lament that they can't understand why their kids made poor choices because "I *told* them what they needed to do."

So how do kids learn? We believe the most meaningful lessons are taught by *experience*, *example*, and *exploration*. We call these the "three E's of parenting." Kids learn by dealing with real-life problems and experiencing the consequences of their decisions, by watching the example of their parents in the way they live, and by being led to explore their hearts and answer the questions "Why do I do the things I do?" and "What's motivating me to make the choices I make?"

As we discuss the three E's, remember our goals as parents: evangelizing and discipling our kids, showing them how to love God and express that love by serving others, helping them become more independent from us every day, equipping them to become good decision makers and problem solvers, and encouraging them to rely on their heavenly Father. With these goals in mind, we must keep asking ourselves, "Is my parenting style helping my kids become the people God designed them to be? Am I teaching them how to become more independent of me? Are they learning to manage problems and face challenges? Am I leading them in the direction of the heavenly Father?"

This chapter may require many of you to reevaluate your ideas about how your children learn and mature. And if you're like Michelle and me, this may also mean making some big adjustments.

## The First E—Experience

### LEE'S BOX

If you have kids, then you have toys that need batteries. My wife, Charlotte, constantly reminded our daughters to turn off the toys so the batteries wouldn't wear out. But like many of our other well-intentioned instructions, this one seemed to land on deaf ears. Charlotte thought about the three E's and decided to add some experiential learning to the mix. When the batteries in a toy ran dead and the girls asked her to replace them, she said, "You know, replacing batteries gets really expensive, but I have some chores you can do to earn more batteries if you'd like." She had them earning batteries by doing things like helping to clean out the car, watering the plants, and folding clothes. One day, she happened to overhear our oldest daughter, Ella, telling her younger sister, Molly, "Turn off that toy so you won't have to work for more batteries!" That brought a smile to Charlotte's face.

Lee's story about the batteries is a great example of using experience to teach a lesson. Do you think the result would have been the same if Charlotte had just told the girls about the cost and inconvenience of buying new batteries? Of course, no. Yet many of us find that allowing life experiences to teach lessons makes us feel uncomfortable. If you're a rescuer, your tendency is to try to prevent your child from making a mistake in the first place or to step in and "fix" a difficult situation so he won't have to face the pain of negative consequences. If you're a dictator, your tendency is to control the experience by giving precise instructions and insisting on prompt obedience. But neither of these approaches allows children the freedom to make choices and experience the consequences of their decisions so they can learn how to make better choices in the future.

Picture your kids as little scientists constantly running experiments and testing out different ideas and concepts as they mature. If you're like us, you'll want your kids to do these experiments in your "laboratory" where you can walk with them and provide appropriate boundaries. Parental supervision is very important. But if you run your laboratory in such a way that your kids don't get to conduct actual experiments, you may be postponing an important process. Trial and error doesn't work if we micromanage the trial or rescue our kids from the error.

Many of us fear mistakes so much that we don't allow our kids to have the kinds of experiences they need to mature. Some parents really enjoy taking care of almost everything for their kids. Other parents like the sense of control it brings. But what will happen when these kids leave home one day? They will probably discover there is a lot they don't know how to do. They may never have learned how to wash their clothes, make dinner, manage their finances, or have a mutually respectful relationship with a roommate or spouse. Preventing mistakes and rescuing from consequences postpones the learning process. Our teens will still have to conduct experiments to learn, but they won't be able to conduct them while they are living in our homes where we can guide them and where the stakes are relatively low. Managing your children's lives for them may seem like a loving or expeditious approach, but it can actually be a handicap. A wise person once said, "Don't handicap your kids by making their lives too easy."

## MICHELLE'S BOX

I have a friend who loves serving her family. She feels most useful and productive when she does their laundry, makes their dinners, picks up school supplies, gets their cars repaired, and so on. After attending one of our classes, she realized she had taken on too many of her kids' responsibilities. This became clear when her oldest son went to college and called her in frustration. He'd done his laundry for the first time and everything had turned pink. He was irritated with *her* for not teaching him how to do it correctly!

While serving our families is admirable, some of us use that as an excuse to get things done our way. Getting things done quickly and efficiently may lower our anxiety level, but it often comes at the cost of teaching our kids necessary skills. Even after my friend was convinced that she needed to give back some responsibilities to her family, she had a difficult time letting go. She had to learn how to tolerate mistakes and inefficiency in order for her children to become more independent of her.

Allowing your children to have the kinds of experiences that will help them grow may be a big challenge for you, but this is easier when you keep the long-term goal in mind: raising mature and responsible adults. It can even be fun to walk with your kids through experiences to see how they process and respond to problems. You may be surprised how resourceful they become.

The principle of experience includes four important elements.

1. *Children need problems to solve.* Kids will run into problems. That's a given. The question is how we will handle those issues when they do. When we solve our children's problems for them, we have taken away opportunities for them to learn. Kids are much more likely to learn problem-solving skills when they are given the opportunity to struggle with actual problems.

2. *Children should be encouraged to try to solve as many of these problems as they can on their own.* Kids need to use their brains. Good decision-making skills are honed by practice and repetition. You may be surprised to learn that valuable neural connections are formed when a child struggles to find solutions. You can help your child grow by encouraging him to

consider his own possible solutions first and by being a sounding board for him. In addition to maximizing the learning process, your child will become more confident in his ability to solve problems.

3. *Children should be allowed to learn from the results.* When a child makes a good or a bad choice, the consequence of that choice will reinforce the experience. That's critical. Without a consequence, no real learning is derived from the experience. When the result is negative, following through with a consequence will speak much louder than a verbal critique of what went wrong. When a good choice results in a positive consequence, don't take it for granted. It is important to recognize your kids' victories just as much as it is to respond to their mistakes.

   Research in education shows it takes four statements of praise for every criticism to maintain on-task behavior in a child. I decided to try this with my boys over the course of one day. I was surprised to realize how much more likely I was to offer correction than praise. Try journaling or logging your ratio of criticism to praise for one day. You may find, as I did, that it is more natural for you to point out the things you'd like your children to change than it is to recognize what you appreciate about them.

4. *Children need support for their efforts.* Kids need encouragement—especially when they make mistakes. Encouraging their efforts gives them enormous confidence. This shows that no mistake is too big to be redeemed and that you believe in their ability to get back up and keep trying. Sometimes, what you *don't* say is as important as what you do say. Don't try to drive home a lesson with an "I told you so" or an accusing "What in the world were you thinking?" Those kinds of statements deflate your kids and cause them to shift the focus from their poor choice to your unkind words.

Please understand that we are not recommending "hands-off" parenting. We cannot give our kids every possible choice. We wouldn't let a ten-year-old drive to the store or allow a three-year-old to sharpen knives. We have to measure the freedom we give our kids according to their age and level of maturity. But it is possible to balance our God-given authority while giving our kids the choices and experience they need to grow and mature. Setting the boundaries within which we allow our kids to make choices is the job of a good, balanced authority.

## LEE'S BOX

I had an experience with age-appropriate choices when our family went to dinner one evening. The server brought the kids a coloring sheet with the children's menu items on it. Our daughter Ella, who was three at the time, said she wanted the pasta dish we knew she didn't like. But it was at the top of the menu and looked appealing to her. We reminded her she hadn't eaten her pasta the last time she'd ordered it, but she insisted, "I want the pasta."

It would have been easy to refuse and order something else for her, but my wife and I decided to let her make the choice. As you might expect, when the server set the pasta in front of her, she scrunched up her face and said, "I don't *like* it!" We were so tempted to say, "Of course you don't like it. You didn't like it last time. That's why we told you not to order it." We were also tempted to call the server over to order something else. But we decided to use our Parenting by Design skills. We empathically said, "Oh, wow, we're so sorry you aren't happy with your meal. That must be tough! Your mom and I are sad for you. But that's what you ordered for dinner. What do you think you're going to do?"

For the rest of the meal, Ella picked at her pasta and didn't eat much. When dinner was over, we got a carryout container and took the pasta home. Predictably, later that evening, she said she was hungry and wanted something to eat. We knew she hadn't quite learned everything she could from the experience, so we said, "Well, we still have your pasta from the restaurant." We let her deal with the consequences of her choice, not to be mean or manipulative but rather to reinforce the lesson that the choices she makes will affect the quality of her life.

I'll admit it was tough. But we thought it was more important to allow Ella to have a mildly painful lesson so she could learn that her choices have real meaning.

What a great example of an age-appropriate experience! Lee and Charlotte didn't give Ella every choice; she couldn't have a milkshake for dinner, for example. But everyone, even a three-year-old, can learn by being given a measure of control over his or her life. Lee had to get out of his comfort zone and allow Ella to be a little hungry when she didn't eat the pasta. In doing so, his daughter received a valuable message: her choices are important. That's a necessary lesson to learn. Interestingly, Lee said that the next time they went to the same restaurant, Ella looked at the menu and started to circle the pasta. Then she stopped, looked up, laughed, crossed out the pasta, and ordered a pizza.

## Letting Children Fail

As our kids were growing up, Michelle and I believed we could solve most of their problems better and faster than they could. And we assumed we *should* step in and solve problems for them because that was our job as parents. But we've come to realize that when we rescued our children from difficulties or dictated how they should handle a problem, we were just postponing opportunities for them to grow. In addition, we were sending them negative implied messages.

First, we realized our rescuing and dictating delayed their development from childhood to adulthood. They needed to develop relationally, intellectually, and morally. We'll talk more in chapter 10 about God's intricate process for growing kids into adults, but one thing is certain: advancing from one developmental stage to the next requires hands-on experience. Without age-appropriate experiences, it is very difficult for a child to grow and mature.

Second, rescuing our kids from pain or dictating exactly what they should do implied that we considered them to be incapable or incompetent—a really harsh message for a kid to receive. We found that when our children were denied hands-on experience in problem solving and decision making, they were likely to carry a tentative mind-set into adulthood—being frightened that any mistake will reveal they don't know what they're doing. This is an unfortunate by-product of micromanagement.

Third, when Michelle and I rescued our boys from consequences, we realized we sent the implied message they could do whatever they wanted without having to consider the *results* of their poor choices. Imagine the shock when they left home and realized there are consequences for poor behavior and choices. We would have much preferred for them to learn about "sowing and reaping" while they lived with us.

Interestingly, it has been proven that giving kids more experiences is also physiologically important. When scientists began looking at kids' brains by using functional MRIs, they discovered that experience helped build and strengthen neural pathways and helped their brains mature.[8] When we deprive our children of problem-solving and decision-making experiences, we deprive their brains of the opportunity to build those neural pathways.

## MICHELLE'S BOX

For many of us, letting our kids struggle seems like an unloving thing to do. We're programmed to believe if there's something we can do to help our kids, we should do it. Withholding assistance can feel mean-spirited. For example, I can remember several times when our boys would tell me at ten o'clock at night they needed some supplies for a project due the next day. Often, I felt compelled to drop everything and go to the store. Can you see how this enabled irresponsible behavior? I had to learn to say, "I'll be more than happy to help you get the supplies for your projects when you give me some advance notice. I can't go tonight, but you're really creative. I bet you can come up with some alternative."

It was amazing to see how resourceful they could be when I didn't jump in and solve the problem for them. One time, Bob took a poster off his wall and used the back of it to do a school project. But there were also times when the project didn't get done. This pulled me out of my comfort zone, but I knew that sacrificing a good grade was necessary for them to learn important lessons, such as time management, delayed gratification, and how to be respectful of others. I realized that allowing them to make a poor grade was really one of the *most* loving things I could do for them.

One experience that will equip our kids for the future is to assign chores. Lately, it seems our culture has drifted away from the practice of giving chores. Maybe it's because kids are busy with school, sports, and social activities and we feel we have to protect their time. My guess is we haven't thought much about the valuable life lessons regular chores can teach, and it's just easier to do it ourselves. But kids can learn time management, teamwork, and how to accomplish age-appropriate responsibilities from chores. By the time they leave home, they can learn to do their own laundry, fix their own meals, manage their own schedule, balance a checkbook, and so on. We can help prepare them to live on their own.

When we first gave chores to our kids, Bob chose to cook dinner for the family once a week. We thought it was a great idea. He started out somewhat reluctantly, but soon his enthusiasm grew. He talked to the butcher or the fish vendor to learn about the different cuts and to get ideas on how to prepare them. Of course, being a teenage boy, he served a lot of meals that were heavy on the protein part of the nutritional pyramid. I remember one dinner in particular that consisted of a shrimp appetizer, chicken Caesar salad, and crawfish. But that was okay. We avoided the temptation to give advice on how to make it perfect. He was proud of what he accomplished, he learned a new skill, and he was excited about making unique meals for us to enjoy. He felt like an integral part of the family and a team player. He learned that adult responsibilities weren't all drudgery. Over time, he became quite the chef and discovered he had a God-given talent and love for cooking.

We rob our kids when we don't allow them to work through the challenges of balancing their time, learning new skills, and fulfilling responsibilities. These are things we all have to learn as adults. While it's difficult to learn how to prioritize and manage our time, the best training ground is our home.

The hard part of experiential learning is that our kids will eventually run some bad "experiments." We know they will fail from time to time, and we have to be prepared when it happens. Recognizing that our job as parents is to respond well, we should take the longest possible view of our kids' poor choices and the consequences of those choices. Looking past momentary embarrassment and realizing that mistakes give your child an opportunity to learn will help you get through it. When your kids develop their problem-solving and decision-making skills in these situations, they will be better equipped to do it on their own without you. That's a positive outcome, even if the immediate situation appears discouraging to them and to you.

Taking a longer view would have helped a lot when we dropped our son off at his treatment programs. At the time, we did not consider how these might be blessings in disguise because they felt like the worst experiences of our lives. But those painful experiences built character and maturity into each of us—not just our son but Michelle and me as well. A lot of good has come out of those very difficult events, although that was not obvious to us at the time.

We're convinced that's why James tells us to "consider it pure joy" when we encounter trials (James 1:2). That doesn't mean God expects us to jump up and down and celebrate things like dropping a child off at a drug treatment center. Trials and tragedies usually aren't joyful when you're in the midst of them. But as the passage explains, the suffering that tests our faith produces perseverance, and perseverance produces maturity when it finishes its work (vv. 3–4). Painful experiences can be gifts from God to make us into the kind of people He designed us to be.

From that perspective, we hinder our children's maturity by rescuing them from problems or by dictating solutions to them. What seems like the most loving thing at the time can ultimately delay their development. Even though it's hard, we encourage parents to look at a struggling child and say, "This experience and consequence can be a great learning opportunity for my child. I will walk with him through it and be as empathetic as I know how to be, but this problem is his and this pain is part of how God is teaching and shaping him."

Michelle recalls how she was tempted to clean up the boys' messes instead of holding them accountable. Frankly, it was easier for her to do it herself. But she thought of their wives having to do the same thing and wondering, "Didn't his mother teach him how to clean up *anything?*" That motivated her to let our kids confront their own cleaning "issues." That's taking the long view!

## Making the Most of Experiences

As we said before, allowing our kids to walk through the consequences of their decisions is crucial for turning experiences into productive learning processes. We will discuss consequences in detail in chapters 12 and 13. What we'd like to stress now is that when you do deliver consequences, remember to give them lovingly and with empathy. Years from now, we don't want our kids to remember us as being mean-spirited and harsh. We want them to remember that even when we didn't support their behavior, we remained supportive of them. Delivering consequences without empathy can undermine the bond between parents and children, while disciplining with love actually strengthens it.

## Control versus Influence

Letting your kids fail may feel like giving up control. Many of us imagine we can and should tightly control our children because we know what's best for them and we know how they should do things. Even when we realize we don't have nearly the control over our kids that we think we do, it can still be difficult to give up our *perception* of control. For example, most of us will discover that we can't control our kids' attitudes, emotions, or interests. As they get older, we also find we have less control over the friends they choose, whom they see at school, or what they do when they are out of sight. In truth, the only things we *can* truly control are our responses to their choices.

The great news is that a parent's response to a child's behavior has a *big* influence on the child's future choices. If we can learn to control and manage our responses to the mistakes our kids are bound to make, we can trade our inflated sense of control for real influence in their lives.

This was challenging for me when my kids made mistakes—especially disobedience or rebellion. I got angry. That's a natural reaction, but when I expressed my anger in belittling ways, I created a whole new issue for my family. The poor choice my son made wasn't the focal point anymore; instead, everyone was focused on my angry reaction. In those moments, I was seen as mean, condescending, or unreasonable. I had lost the opportunity to use my kids' poor choices to teach them anything. However, when I learned to express my anger in healthier, more empathetic ways, my boys were more likely to let me walk with them through the issue. Empathy was the key.

Obviously, that's easier said than done. If you tend to respond to poor choices with anger, sarcasm, lectures, or personal attacks, don't deal with a difficult situation in the heat of the moment. You can always tell a child, "That was a poor choice and there will be a consequence, but I can't tell you what it is right now." You don't have to deliver a consequence on the spot. Sometimes, it's a good idea to delay consequences and revisit the issue later when you can be more empathetic. Remember empathy is the glue that holds all the parenting principles together. It is absolutely worth the effort to postpone consequences until you can muster the necessary empathy.

Also important is knowing that empathy isn't the same as sympathy. Sympathy is feeling sorry for someone's situation. But empathy requires much more from us. Empathy is respectfully listening to someone with a desire to understand his or her feelings and perspectives. However, desiring to understand someone's feelings and perspectives isn't the same as agreeing with them or approving their behavior. You can understand another person's perspective without agreeing with it. Empathy acknowledges the child's point of view even if it is different from yours, but that doesn't require you to accept or condone his behavior. Your main concern is to understand how your kids see and experience the world. Communicating with them in an empathetic way provides the safe environment they need to risk revealing what they truly think and feel. This is a big step toward "knowing" your kids. We will discuss some practical ways to communicate empathy in chapters 14 and 15.

## The Second E—Example

Your kids watch and learn a lot about life from you. This is an intimidating thought, but your example is also their first curriculum about God. From an early age, they will hear stories about their "heavenly Father" and their "brothers and sisters in Christ." The primary reference point they have for those terms is family. That means that if you are a judgmental parent, they are likely to see God as a judgmental, condemning Father. If you're a rescuer, they are likely to think that God wants everyone to be happy and doesn't want anyone to suffer consequences. But the balance of truth and love demonstrated by a counselor parent paves the way for children to understand both God's righteousness *and* His grace. And while we recognize that being an example of God is an impossible standard and that every parent will fall short, don't let this defeat you. Use His example to guide and encourage you. Trust Him to equip you, knowing He is bigger than your parenting mistakes.

A parent's example also is the children's primary illustration of what it means to be an adult. They have friends, they see hundreds of TV channels, and they have access to the Internet. But you as parents are still the most important influence in your children's lives. One of the greatest gifts you can give your children is to live a life that demonstrates the values you'd like them to adopt.

So what does being a good example look like? The place to start is with humility. No matter what kind of parent you are, the simple truth is you will make mistakes. When you do, it's important to be willing to say to your kids, "You know, I blew it when I said that. I'm sorry. Will you forgive me?" This is difficult for some parents because they see it as weakness or as undermining their authority. But humility isn't a sign of weakness; it's an example of strength. If your kids emulate you in just this one area, they will have learned a life skill that truly honors God.

You also want to be an example of a parent who faces and solves his problems. If you show your kids that *you* can learn from your experiences, they are more likely to want to try it too. Show them how you deal with problems constructively—not avoiding, ignoring, or overreacting to them but handling them with confidence and faith. They are likely to pick up on your approach to hardships and difficulties and incorporate your approach in their own lives.

Your ability to give and receive empathy is also an important example for your children. And giving and receiving empathy is not only a great example; it is also physiologically important. Recent research shows that "mirror" neurons develop more readily in the brains of young children who receive empathy and that the newly developed mirror neurons give them the capacity to offer the same kind of empathy to others.[9] In other words, when kids see empathy in action from the people who most directly influence them, they become more capable of being empathetic themselves.

Also of importance is showing children how to learn from consequences. They need to see how adults model this learning process. When you do this, your kids will see that mistakes are not the end of the world but are opportunities to learn and grow. I got a speeding ticket once—I was going twenty-six in a twenty-mile-per-hour zone (embarrassing, I know), and my kids were in the car with me. I wanted to rant and rave about the police officer who pulled me over, the obstructed road sign, and everything else—except for my poor judgment. But I realized I could be a better example if I stayed calm and accepted the consequences. I knew that saying, "Okay, I messed up, and now I have to deal with the consequences," would demonstrate to them how to own up to mistakes and accept the consequences. In this case, I would have to sit in front of my computer screen for several hours taking a driver's education course. But if I had whined about it, blamed the cop, or refused to do the work, that would have sent a different message. I wanted my kids to learn from consequences. That meant I had to be willing to do the same.

Another gift you can give your children is to let them see you focusing on your strengths. God has given each of us gifts, and parents should take the time to uncover their children's unique God-given gifts. And it makes sense that if you want to be a good example in this respect, you should model the process of discovering and enjoying the gifts God has given to *you*. Studies done by the Gallup organization have shown that people who are at the top of their fields in business, sports, government, and ministry have one major characteristic in common— and it is not an Ivy League education. The common thread that runs through the lives of people who excel in their professions is that they discovered what they were good at and they did it. What a novel idea! Yet this is exactly where many parents get it wrong with their kids. Parents often try to make artists into baseball players or engineers into concert pianists. Some of us don't figure out where our gifts are until we're well into adulthood, because we're trying to excel in areas that are important to our parents. If we can show our kids how to be the individuals they were designed to be at an earlier age, we can give them a great head start in life. Try to model for your kids how you focus on your strengths and help them discover the gifts God designed especially for them.

## The Third E—Exploration

Encouraging self-reflection and insight is the goal of exploration. Let's assume your child has made a mistake and suffered a consequence. You want him to develop the insight necessary to get to the heart of the issue and answer the questions "Why did I make that choice?" What was I hoping to find?" "What desire motivated me to take that risk or make that mistake?" If a child can learn to answer these questions and become adept at self-exploration, he or she will have a gift that will keep on giving for a lifetime. Many of us never truly understand what motivates us.

Maybe we don't ask ourselves the deep questions because we are afraid of the answers. Self-examination can be painful because many times our choices are motivated by insecurity or pride. But when we recognize our triggers and weaknesses, we are less likely to react impulsively and better able to respond in healthier ways.

Exploration will help your kids uncover and then let go of the sin that motivates them to make poor decisions. Remember Adam in the garden? God asked questions to encourage self-exploration. He knew the answers, but He wanted Adam to think about the fact that he was hiding and to consider what had happened to make him want to hide in the first place. Adam had to come face-to-face with the truth that he had not trusted God but had sought to be his own god instead. Being questioned by his loving, empathetic heavenly Father gave Adam the insight, freedom, and strength to leave the garden and try again, secure in the knowledge that, despite his rebellion and the consequences that were due, God still loved him.

You can encourage that kind of self-exploration in your children by following God's example. Be careful not to fall into several common traps, however. Many times, I have prejudged what I believe to be the heart issues when my kids have made a mistake. I am inclined to jump to fix-it mode right away, and exploration is difficult when I have an agenda in mind. In order to do exploration well, I have to consciously set aside my predisposition and judgment and ask open-ended questions that encourage my kids to explore their motivations. Often, I discovered there was a lot more going on inside my sons than what I had originally assumed. But even if I was correct in my initial assessment, I was not the one who needed to know how to find the answers to the questions. I need to ask the questions and guide the process so my kids can find the answers within themselves. That is the skill I want them to learn. But I nip that learning in the bud when I try to prove I was right about what happened. As a former dictator, the tendency to be right sometimes means I turn *self*-examination into *cross*-examination. I stop asking open-ended questions and start trying to prove my point by asking closed questions that will lead to an admission that supports my assumptions. This approach will cause a child to clam up or lash out almost immediately. I had to learn to suspend judgment and let the self-examination process work.

To do exploration well, choose the right time. Trying to do exploration in the heat of the moment probably isn't the best choice. It's too easy for your tone to become accusatory and your child to become defensive. Choose a time when both of you are calm and able to talk comfortably, and ask those open-ended questions. "What was that like? How did that feel? What were you thinking about? Tell me how it happened." Those kinds of questions require your children to think through their behavior. Be careful about your body language because kids will pick up on unspoken judgments. Your tone is also very important. Even when you say all the right words, your tone of voice can convey sarcasm, judgment, or rebuke.

Use silence as your ally; it's a vastly underrated helper. Although you will be tempted, try not to fill in conversational gaps with *your* thoughts or *your* words. Allow time for your children to process and formulate a response. They are likely to need some time and silence to do that. There is also a good chance they will respond to some of your questions with "I don't know." That's okay, because in all likelihood, they really don't know. They may need some time to think it through and develop insight.

Even young children can learn from exploration, though our expectations for them should be a little different. They may not always know why they did something, and they may not be able to express their thoughts in abstract terms the way older kids can. Still, it's important to take them through the process of exploration. You may have to provide the words for them by describing the event and the emotions you are observing, such as follows: "You are very angry because your sister took your toy away. Is that right?" This will help kids learn to identify their feelings. It will also become easier for them to understand and explain their struggles as they grow.

Resist the temptation to give your kids solutions right away. Instead, encourage them by providing just enough help for them to come up with ideas of their own. Problem solving is a skill they will need in life. When kids come up with solutions, they will be more invested in carrying them out. They also will be better equipped to deal with the next situation that comes around.

Don't end the exploration process without pointing your children toward the eternal perspective. Assist them in understanding that every problem can be redeemed, and encourage them to look at the longest possible view of the situation. You're helping your kids understand that whatever happened, it isn't hopeless. This is a great opportunity to say things like "Man, that sounds like a tough situation. What do you think you are going to do?" "We believe in you. I know this is difficult. Let me know if you'd like some help thinking it through." In the grand scheme of things, everything is a learning experience, even if it is painful at the time.

We've also found it helpful to do some self-exploration ourselves before entering an exploration time with our kids. As parents, we have insecurities that motivate us. Are we willing for God to shine His light into our hearts in the same way we want Him to shine it into our kids? After looking inside herself, a mom in one of our groups made an honest observation. She said she often found herself "sacrificing my kids to other parents' expectations." This kind of insight takes courage and humility. Approach exploration with the goal of allowing God to speak truth not only into your child's heart but into yours as well.

## Bringing It Home

Our primary goal is to equip our children to become mature Christians who love God and other people and who become adept problem solvers and decision makers. To do that, we have to accept that often the most loving thing we can do for them is to walk with them as they experience the consequences of their choices, even when that doesn't feel very loving. When they learn from the three E's—experience, example, and exploration—we will find that we don't have to nag and lecture like we used to. Providing a safe and supportive atmosphere to explore their thoughts and feelings using empathy and reflective listening makes it much more likely that our kids will allow us to walk with them through the tough issues of life. In the process, we help our children become the people God designed them to be.

# CHAPTER 5

# WHO'S IN CHARGE AROUND HERE?

Aaron and Jennie wanted the best for their daughter Claire. They knew a good high school résumé was important to get into a prestigious college. They also knew this didn't just happen; it required years of preparatory work. Over the years, they pushed Claire to excel in school and extracurricular activities—the ones she would need in order to be a "success." Aaron and Jennie sacrificed a lot of time and energy to help Claire lay the groundwork for her future.

Early in her life, Claire sensed how important her achievements were to her parents. She wanted to make them proud of her. Whether it was her grades, sports, cheerleading, or clubs, she did it all and excelled at most. But sometimes she neglected more mundane responsibilities because she knew she could count on her parents to bend over backward to make sure she overachieved on the "important stuff."

For example when Claire rushed off to school and left her room in a mess, her mother would clean it up because she knew Claire would be exhausted when she came home. Claire's back-to-back activities were often on different sides of town, so her parents took turns leaving work early to drive her from one to the other. When Claire remembered the night before a club meeting that she'd signed up to bring brownies, her mother would drop everything, go to the store, and make the brownies so Claire could work on her homework instead.

So who really was running Aaron and Jenny's household? It was Claire. Her needs came first, and her parents formed their schedule around hers. Her parents' desire for success led them to sacrifice their time, money, and energy for the goals they had for Claire. That may sound noble at first, but a closer look at the role of the central authority will show you how turning the hierarchy in the home upside down actually results in less growth and maturity, less preparedness for the world, and the possibility of a serious case of entitlement on the part of the children. So what is a proper biblical authority structure for parents and children?

## Central Authority

The undeniable fact is that God expects parents to lead the family. In fact, He spelled out a hierarchy designed for healthy family functioning: The husband is to be the loving, self-sacrificing head of the wife and kids. With this authority comes the most challenging task of all: to love his wife the way Christ loves the church (Eph. 5:23). Talk about a high calling!

Next, the wife is to be intimately involved in and consulted on family decisions. (See Eph. 5:21; 1 Peter 3:7.) Just because she is subject to the husband's headship doesn't mean she has no authority. In reality, lots of child-raising responsibilities are delegated to Mom, and Dad must support her in those tasks.

Finally, children are to obey their parents and learn from the loving, empathetic relationship that develops with them. (See Eph. 6:1–4.) God designed the family in such a way that parents are to function as a team of true, loving, central authorities. This lays the foundation for everyone to fulfill his or her responsibilities to the family with love rather than selfishness or pride. (See Eph. 5:21–6:4.)

Parents must learn the dynamics of exercising authority *together*. Intuitively, kids will learn to master the divide-and-conquer approach to dealing with authority. They will quickly recognize the weaknesses in the parental team and learn how to pit Mom against Dad when it works to their advantage. For example, if Mom has a particular way of dealing with problems and Dad has another, the children will learn to choose which one is better for them as each individual situation crops up. They can run to the rescuer to avoid consequences and to the dictator when they need a problem solved.

Kids are much more likely to learn how to solve problems and face consequences when their parents are united in their approach and fully supportive of each other. These parents are able to provide clearer boundaries and a greater sense of security to their kids. This may require parents to have team meetings from time to time in order to work together. Ideally, you'll discuss these difficult parenting issues in private so you can agree on boundaries and deliver effective consequences as a unit. Even if you don't have time to consult one another before each issue, you've got to be supportive of the other parent and keep your disagreements private and behind closed doors.

Michelle remembers times when our boys would come to her complaining that I had been "mean" to them. She would ask what happened and then ask me for an explanation. We would discuss the situation in front of the kids, where they could observe and take advantage of the widening cracks in our team. After seeing the futility of trying to work separately, we now make the effort to get on the same page with each other in private first. Likewise, if you sense some conflict between you and your spouse about how to handle an issue with your kids, put the issue on hold and talk it out between yourselves privately. *Then* talk to the kids about it. They will recognize the unity and have a much greater respect for the consequences you present to them.

This is where balance becomes one of your most valuable assets. One of the great benefits of being a team is that Mom and Dad usually have different skills, strengths, and weaknesses, and you are stronger together than you are separately. When you learn to balance your strengths and weaknesses and work together, you will become a well-rounded and effective team.

## LEE'S BOX

I often see couples in my practice that have trouble balancing their different approaches to parenting. My advice is to be a team. The rescuer can learn a lot about boundaries from the dictator, and the dictator can learn about bonding from the rescuer. Openly discussing the issues and respectfully listening to each other can lead to true team unity and a balanced parenting approach. This approach teaches spouses to trust each other and to trust the Holy Spirit to guide them in the discussion. This also requires each parent to endure some anxiety and stress as they learn to listen to their spouse's point of view rather than defending their own. Interestingly, I have found that parents who have learned to do this will improve their relationship with each other because they learn to appreciate the strengths of their partner. They learn to draw strength from their relationship rather than working against one another.

There is a tendency on the part of some couples to try to balance the way they exercise authority by being the exact opposite of their spouse. If one parent is a dictator, the other might become more of a rescuer in an effort to balance the harshness of the dictator. For obvious reasons, this does not work. Imagine a rescuer mom who faces her crying kids after Dad has really let them have it. She recognizes the harshness of Dad's discipline and she just can't bear to see her kids in pain, so she takes them to get some ice cream. This implies that Dad overdid it and she can be counted on to help them get over the trauma. She may be completely unaware of the message she sends, but the kids get it clearly. What do you think they are going to do next time they make a bad choice?

Michelle and I often found ourselves trying to balance each other this way. I was on the dictatorial end of the parental teeter-totter, and Michelle was on the rescuing end. The problem was that our kids sat in the middle, keenly observing the dynamic between us. They would run to one end of the teeter-totter or the other depending on which parenting style best suited their purposes at the time. That's not the kind of balance we're talking about!

We recognize it is not always easy for parents to come to an agreement about what to do when they're faced with difficult parenting problems, especially when they are divorced. A good balance is not easy to find. So what do you do if you find yourself disagreeing with your spouse and unable to reach a balanced decision? If the problem is a recurring one that never seems to get resolved, it may be time to seek counseling. If one of the parties doesn't want to go to counseling and refuses to modify his or her style, the only option left is to prayerfully parent the best way you know how. You cannot control what your ex-spouse does or says, but you can control yourself. Your prayer can be that God will help your kids recognize you are parenting them the way He parents all of us—with unconditional love and appropriate discipline.

## Avoiding a Void

Even though most parents know they are supposed to be the central authorities in their homes, many parents, like Claire's, find themselves being held hostage by their children's agendas. Unintentionally, the kids' activities become the central focus of the family's time and energy. With the number of activities available to kids these days, and the subtle competition among parents for the recognition that comes with having kids that do well at these activities, it's a common temptation to want your kids to participate in as many things as possible. This is a major reason many families are stressed and parents feel out of control.

Let's look at the case of Aaron and Jennie. When kids get overly involved in outside activities, the main objective of the family becomes getting the kids to and from all their activities, making sure they have all the equipment and supplies they need, and finding their kids any outside help they need to excel. But when the child's needs begin to set the whole family's agenda, the child becomes the de facto central authority. The child fills the authority void because we have allowed— and even encouraged—his or her interests and agendas to take center stage. All this activity comes at a great price. How? There is very little time and energy left just to be a family. We sacrifice teaching our kids how to be regular participants and contributors to the family. Relaxing and talking together, eating dinner together, and being responsible for regular chores are ways we establish a healthy family environment. Spending quality time together reinforces the idea that we are better off pooling individual efforts for the benefit of all. Among other benefits, we are preparing our kids to be members of the church, where individuals are called to exercise their particular gifts for the mutual good. This is important because our culture has replaced the virtue of working together in community with an emphasis on rugged individuality. We were designed to work together, not separately.

Putting children at the center of the family and letting life revolve around them also gives the leadership position to those who are less experienced, less knowledgeable, and less mature than we are. Kids in this position don't usually assume the leadership position well. They often develop either a sense of entitlement or a dependence on their parents. Entitlement grows when we continually put our kids' activities and desires above our own. We expect appreciation but rarely get it. Rather, we cultivate an expectation that they are the most important members of the family. Dependence develops when we're successful as dictators. We end up with compliant kids who don't know how to take care of themselves or make their own decisions. And either way, we have created a problem rather than solving one; we have children who leave home either thinking the world owes them everything or looking for a new someone to be the authority in their lives and tell them what to do. The best way to avoid entitlement or dependence is for parents to reassert themselves as empathetic, effective central authorities.

## Exercising Authority

An even more subtle way children indirectly acquire the role of central authority is when parenting decisions are shaped by a fear of discipline or causing pain. When parents fail to exercise their authority because they can't stand to see their kids suffer consequences or because they are afraid their kids will be mad at them, the kids have become the authorities in the home. These fearful parents resort to pleading, bargaining, or whining to get their kids to do what they want, but these approaches undermine their authority and rarely get the responses they are seeking.

Some parents are so afraid of being disliked by their kids that they fail to establish reasonable boundaries for the kids' behavior. These parents rationalize with comments like "Well, they were going to do it anyway, so I thought they might as well do it where I can keep an eye on them." What's sad is that the effort to convince their children to like them usually results in disrespect and entitlement instead.

Still other parents are afraid to exercise their authority because they think that enforcing boundaries with consequences will damage their child's self-esteem. They believe every experience must be a positive one or their child will become discouraged and lose heart. But one of the reasons God gives people trials is to build perseverance, maturity, and confidence. Parents who believe in their children and support them in their struggles without rescuing will find that godly self-esteem is a natural by-product of the process of struggling through discipline. (See James 1:2–4; Rom. 5:3–5.)

In contrast to the parents who are afraid to exercise authority, other parents exercise it too harshly. These parents run the family like a drill sergeant, barking out orders and expecting everyone to jump at their commands. They often insist on "first-time obedience," expecting their kids to obey every command without challenge, excuse, or delay.

While we all want our kids to obey the first time we ask, the dictatorial approach sends a message that we aren't willing to listen to our kids. It emphasizes our power and authority over the value of having an authentic relationship with our kids. This makes obedience difficult for rebellious kids and mechanical for compliant kids. In neither case is the child learning from his or her experiences because the parents are forcing their will on the child rather than walking beside them and using the experiences to shape their character. Far from having the positive influence they desire, an overbearing parenting style can cause kids to become preoccupied with the power disparity. As a result, many kids can't wait to get out from underneath this power structure as soon as possible. In the meantime, they will look for passive/aggressive ways to exert their own power.

As parents, it is time to reevaluate what it truly means to exercise godly authority. This is not being permissive or domineering but rather being balanced as God is balanced. He will help us learn to exercise our authority well and how to maintain a careful balance between truth and love. God expects and equips us to exercise our power empathetically and judiciously, with the overarching goal of encouraging each member of the family to grow into the person He designed them to be. Pray for the wisdom to be that kind of parent.

## Different Strokes for Different Folks

One of the interesting aspects of exercising godly authority in the home is learning to recognize the different personalities, gifts, and needs of your kids. God gave Michelle and me an introverted artist and an outgoing counselor. To be effective as central authorities over our kids, we couldn't have one set of hard-and-fast rules. We had to consider each son's personality and set boundaries and deliver discipline in the most effective way for each of them. You'll notice this with your kids too; one child will have a set of strengths and weaknesses that often differs substantially from your other children. You will have to construct an environment for each child, using choices, consequences, and empathy to maximize their unique style of learning and enable them to figure out what it is God put them on the earth to do.

Be aware that at various times in your children's lives, they will think this idea of different rules for different kids is a double standard. "That's not fair" is a common complaint, especially at certain developmental stages when they are especially drawn to the concept of fairness. Don't give up! You can use even those conflicts as opportunities to teach your kids that fairness is not a defining principle to live by and that sometimes it is necessary for parents to do what is best for their kids rather than what seems fair. You know from experience that life is not always fair, and this is a lesson better taught by you in the security of your home than for your children to have to learn it in the cruel, harsh world. Besides, the family isn't a justice system. The family is an environment in which each person can grow into the person God designed him or her to be.

You may need to set up different boundaries and privileges for each of your children. Some kids are able to balance schoolwork and extracurricular activities without much difficulty. They don't need rigid boundaries to learn how to manage their time. When they ask to go hang out with friends, you'll usually feel free to say, "Sure, I'd love for you to be able to do that. As soon as you finish your homework, you can go hang out with them." Other kids, even in the same family, may struggle to use their time wisely enough to get the grades they are capable of and still have time to do the things they want. As a parent of these kids, you might have to take a stronger approach by saying, "You know I'd love for you to hang out with your friends, but as your parent, I don't think it would be very responsible to allow you to do that right now. Why don't you work on your homework, and we can talk about it again after we see some improvement in your grades?" Same family, same request, but different approaches. Why? Because different kids have different needs for structure and boundaries. The good, central authority recognizes the need for different approaches. And you can empathize with your children on how difficult it is to be subject to different sets of rules.

Parents sometimes get nervous about it, but there's nothing wrong with exercising your authority on an individual basis. There's no clause in the "parenting handbook" that says you have to have the same rules for each of your kids. They aren't identical, so as you deal with them individually, you can be sensitive to each child's unique design.

## Choices

Giving our kids age-appropriate choices encourages responsibility, growth, and maturity. Remember the garden of Eden? When God created Adam and Eve, He gave them tasks to perform and He established a few basic rules to follow. He set generous boundaries and gave them many choices about significant issues. They had the freedom and opportunity to choose how they would exercise the dominion God gave them. God gave Adam the responsibility of naming the animals. Adam and Eve even had the freedom to respect God's boundaries or not, but either way, these choices carried consequences. God gave them lots of freedom and responsibility, but He also made it clear that His consequences would be commensurate with the way they handled that freedom and responsibility.

Unlike some human parents who have an inflated idea of the amount of control they have over their kids, God really *could* have made Adam and Eve do anything He wanted. He could have forced them to comply with His will. He could have made them robots—programmed to do the right thing at the right time. Instead, He gave them the freedom to exercise their will. He put the forbidden tree in the middle of the garden and told them not to eat from it, but He didn't force them to comply. Because God did not exercise His absolute control, Adam and Eve had the freedom to cross that boundary or not.

We know what happened. They disobeyed, and God delivered the consequences He promised. Although He knew it would happen, it must have broken His heart. But God's response as the ultimate central Authority was not unbalanced. We can learn a lot about parenting rebellious kids from this story. When Adam and Eve violated specific boundaries in Eden, God didn't leave or forsake them. He remained unconditionally bonded to them even as He changed their environment—ushering them out of paradise. He never abandoned the relationship. In spite of their rebellion and the terrible consequences that resulted from it, He sought them out, helped them develop the insight they were going to need outside the garden, and covered their shame with animal skins. Then He gave them another opportunity to obey and to exercise dominion over the new environment He established for them.

That's a great picture of a perfect parent. The ideal parent gives his children reasonable boundaries and understands that they will have to decide whether they are going to respect those boundaries or not. We have to remember we aren't raising robots. We're preparing our kids to be responsible adults in a world full of positive and negative options. We give them choices that will help them become better problem solvers and decision makers. But—and this can be one of the most difficult things we do as parents—we also have to be willing to let them experience the consequences of their choices. When they cross a boundary we have set, they must learn from that wrong decision.

At the same time, we must be sure our kids know that no matter what happens, we are committed to a permanent relationship with them. We will make ourselves available to counsel and walk beside them, especially when they deal with the consequences of poor choices. We will never withdraw our love, even when their choices work against them. We will walk with them through the pain, even when their pain is the result of ignoring boundaries and disobeying rules.

I know of kids whose choices have led them into the criminal justice system. The consequences are daunting, I can tell you. Some of these parents recognized that facing the justice system was the best opportunity these kids might have to understand the concepts of reaping and sowing so they allowed the consequences to do the teaching. At the same time, they wanted their kids to know they were still loved and that Mom and Dad were available to counsel with them about possible options in lawyers, deferred adjudication, pleas, and so forth. But the kids were fully aware that Mom and Dad were not going to take over their issues for them or to throw money at the problems to try to make them go away. In these situations, the parents walked beside their kids, not in front of them. This is terribly difficult to do, but these parents realized that many of the most profound lessons are learned from the most trying circumstances, and they trusted God enough to let Him work on their kids.

Let me add one caveat to this discussion. There are times when the most loving thing is to let your child have some time alone to think about the consequences of his or her actions. Saying we will always be available to counsel with them does not mean we will be at their beck and call twenty-four hours a day, seven days a week. For example, we discovered our son had been making some unauthorized phone calls in the first couple of months of his second rehab stint. At the time, he had earned weekly visiting privileges so we were able to visit him on Saturday nights. But when we learned about the calls, we made some decisions about our support for him. We decided that although we loved him and would miss the visiting time, we would not make the weekly visits until we were certain he was taking his rehab seriously. We didn't abandon him or withdraw our love. We just wanted him to understand the consequences of not following the rules and to become serious about getting sober. That time alone proved to be the turning point for Bob. He realized that, other than family, the only real friend he had left was Jesus.

If we follow God's example, we'll learn to approach our children's choices by seeking to *influence* them rather than trying to *control* them. We'll set them up for success as well as we can, and we'll cultivate their maturity and sense of responsibility. We'll teach them the difference between right and wrong, and we'll try to instill wisdom in them. But we won't take away their freedom to make age-appropriate choices, and we won't spare them from the consequences that result from their choices. And regardless of their choices, we'll stay in the relationship and walk with them through whatever they face. That's what the perfect parent does for us, and that's how He designed us to relate to our kids.

## Respecting Authority

Another aspect of a being a good central authority is teaching our kids about interacting with authority figures. One of the most important things we can teach our children is how to respect the authorities he or she will encounter. Authority is a fact of life for everyone. No matter how independent we think we are, every human being has an authority in his or her life—someone to whom they are accountable. As our kids grow up, they will have parents, teachers, coaches, administrators, and bosses as authority figures. Ultimately, of course, everyone should look to God as his or her authority. No one outgrows the need to be accountable to Him. But God knows the importance of earthly authorities and gave us specific directions for submitting to them. (See Rom. 13:1–7.)

The sixth commandment is about honoring one's father and mother. (See Ex. 20:12.) God saw fit to put respect for parents in His top ten rules! But He has also made it clear throughout Scripture that other anointed leaders—governmental rulers, spiritual authorities, and others—are to be honored for their positions. He even urged believers to respect the authority of ungodly governments, not because those governments were righteous but because they were under His sovereign hand. Respecting authority is more than good advice for family life; it's a key truth from God's Word. Learning this truth will help our children in the short term and enable our families to function more smoothly. But the issue of respect also has bigger, lifelong implications. You are doing a big favor for your kids and saving them a lot of heartache if you teach them respect for authority.

At the same time, it is just as important that those in authority strive to be worthy of the respect due to them. In the long run, authority is only effective when respected, and real respect has to be earned. Dictators may demand respect for themselves and they can sometimes force those under their authority to comply with their will, at least externally. But *earning* respect is far more difficult than simply being demanding. The way we parent our children can cultivate respect or undermine it.

## MICHELLE'S BOX

Ironically, one of the best ways to cultivate respect is to follow through on consequences. While it can be hard to be consistent, how we respond to our children's disobedience has a direct effect on how they perceive our authority. For example, when our kids were little, I liked to take them to the park. This was supposed to be fun, but sometimes, the boys would fight over the swing or refuse to share their toys. I usually responded in one of two ways: I would pull them aside and tell them, "Straighten up right now or we're leaving!" or I would plead, "Come on, guys. We came all the way to the park, and you don't want to have to go home." Neither of these responses cultivated much respect for my authority. After a while, my boys knew I wasn't going to leave, so my threats were disregarded. And my pleading was just as ineffective. It's difficult to respect someone who is begging you to obey!

It would have been much more effective to have given the boys a choice that reflected my boundaries. "Would you rather play nicely or head home?" If they chose to continue arguing, then I should have let the consequence of leaving the park teach the lesson. I should have remained firm and calm and said, "I'm so sorry you guys can't get along. We're going home." And then, of course, I should have loaded them in the car and taken them home. I wouldn't have needed many words. Leaving would have made my point. If the same situation arose in the future, the boys likely would have responded with respect for my authority, because I would have kept my word. Instead, the message that came across is "Mom talks a big game but doesn't really follow through."

Michelle's example illustrates one of the difficulties with following through with consequences. It can be inconvenient and even a little embarrassing to leave the park, especially when you are with friends. But it's far better in the long run to suffer a little inconvenience in the moment if it means you won't deal with the same issue over and over. Remember the most loving thing you can do for your kids doesn't always feel very loving. But being a good, empathetic disciplinarian and enforcing appropriate consequences follows the model of our heavenly Father described in Hebrews 12:5–11. Rather than yanking your kids aside and trying to talk them out of difficult situations, try empathetically delivering good consequences. You probably did want to stay at the park, but delivering the consequence of leaving tells them it is important that they learn to act within the boundaries.

## Bringing It Home

God created families with a particular hierarchy in mind, and parents are at the top of that hierarchy. For dictators, this is a comfortable position. For rescuers afraid of disciplining their kids, it can be more difficult. But a balance of bonding and boundaries is essential to being a godly authority that earns respect by treating his or her kids with respect. A balanced parent sets boundaries, gives age-appropriate choices within those boundaries, and delivers consequences when kids stray.

Kids will sometimes assume the position of authority in a family when the parents cede power to them, either by making the children's activities the most important events of each day or by failing to deliver consequences when they are deserved. Take some time to reflect and pray about your responsibilities and priorities for your family. Is family time sacred, or does it get sacrificed in order to get to the next practice, game, meeting, or event? Do you eat dinner together often, or is life too hectic for that?

Do you lovingly discipline your children when they make poor choices, or are you afraid of their reaction? What about the reaction of other parents? Do you worry that you might be seen as a bad parent if your kids are not doing all the things the other kids are doing? Or do you insist on first-time obedience and fail to consider that it's important for your kids to know the reasons for asking a them to do something? Is your attitude "my way or the highway" where your kids' thoughts, opinions, or reactions are ignored just to get things done?

Take heart! God knows your struggles and your tendencies. Ask for help, and wait to hear. Spend some time with your Bible and look for God's wisdom. He will speak through the words on those pages. Be empathetic and earn the respect of your kids through clear boundaries, consistent consequences, and a willingness to walk with them through the struggles of life.

# CHAPTER 6

# PLEASE FENCE ME IN

Judy struggled with setting boundaries with her teenage son. Each time she told him her expectations, he argued that she was being unfair. Because Judy grew up with parents who dismissed her thoughts and feelings, this hit her in a vulnerable place. She didn't want to do the same thing to her son. So when he got angry with her, she felt guilty and second-guessed her decisions. Sometimes, it just took too much energy to follow through.

Someone has said that "good fences make good neighbors," and this is true in families as well; good boundaries make healthy families. A big part of an effective central authority's responsibility is to set clear boundaries for your children. Boundaries provide security, communicate values, and establish a safe environment for learning.

Research confirms the importance of setting boundaries for children. In one study, researchers let children play on an unfenced field surrounded by busy roads. They observed a lot of anxious behavior in the kids—avoiding the outside edges of the field and gravitating toward the center, for instance. When the kids had to go to the edge of the lot, they did it with a sense of fear. They didn't feel free to run all over the field. Then the researchers put up a fence high enough that the kids couldn't get out and others couldn't get in. With the same kids in the same field, the existence of the fence (a tangible boundary) allowed them to feel free enough to run anywhere they wanted. They ran right up to the fence. They played without fear because they felt safe in their environment. They knew where the limits were. The boundaries actually gave them a *greater* sense of freedom.

Giving kids appropriate boundaries helps them develop a sense of security and a value system and makes them feel safe, just as when we give them physical boundaries. When we establish guidelines for their behavior, we are following God's example. He gives us boundaries for our protection and His glory. His boundaries *are* His value system.

The Bible is full of examples of boundary setting. God's first boundary was established in the garden of Eden when God made the tree of the knowledge of good and evil off limits to Adam and Eve. God gave the Israelites the Ten Commandments and then the Law as ways to reveal His character, keep them safe, and show them what it meant to be truly holy. The book of Proverbs gives parents guidance on setting boundaries for themselves and their children.

God Himself demonstrated the value of boundaries for us. When Jesus was exhausted, He would go away from the crowds—sometimes from His own disciples—to pray and be alone with His Father. Marital, sexual, and relational boundaries are covered by many passages in the New Testament. Throughout the Bible, God makes it clear that His boundaries are a reflection of His love and a guide to help us live more abundantly. (See Heb. 12:8–10.) Don't let anyone tell you that boundaries are unbiblical.

## MICHELLE'S BOX

The importance of boundaries was apparent to me when eleven-year-old Emily and her mother came to the counseling office for help with Emily's anxiety. Within a few minutes I could tell the *mother* was dealing with anxiety as well. Emily was eleven going on twenty-five. She walked into the office with a self-assured swagger and proceeded to interrupt her mom repeatedly as her mom tried to explain the situation. Sheepishly her mother would ask her not to interrupt. Emily would roll her eyes. But Emily's bravado disintegrated into anger and tears when her mom related all the things Emily wanted her mom to buy her. Emily was jealous because her younger sister had gotten a new bedspread. Emily wanted a new bedspread too. Her mother explained that they had redecorated Emily's room a year before and now it was her sister's turn. "But my stuff looks old now!" Emily protested. "At least get me some new pillows!" Her mother seemed completely at a loss for how to handle this strong-willed child. When she tried to reason with her, Emily had a loud rebuttal for every point she made. Exhausted, the mother's resolve began to fade and she finally agreed to consider buying one or two pillows if Emily was "good."

Although she appeared to get her way, this dynamic contributed to Emily's anxiety. She was aware of the control she exercised over her mother, but she also seemed to know, deep down, that she was not prepared to handle this kind of control. When she pushed to find where the boundaries were—and she pushed hard—her mother catered to her demands. Ironically, this *lack* of boundaries is what made Emily anxious. Over time, her mother found the strength to maintain firm boundaries and deliver consequences. Initially, Emily did not like this "new mother," but when her mother remained consistent, Emily's protesting and anxiety began to decline. She knew her boundaries were secure.

## Setting Good Boundaries

Good boundaries are only effective when they are enforced, so you'll need good consequences for the inevitable times when your boundaries are violated. Brainstorm some consequences and have them in mind *before* the violation. We will cover guidelines for giving consequences in chapter 13, but you should know that the two go hand in hand; setting appropriate boundaries will give you the confidence to follow through when consequences are necessary. Your kids will know that you mean what you say. That's an important concept for them because they want to know that their parents can be trusted.

What are some other tips for setting good boundaries? It's a good idea to start with conservative boundaries and then gradually extend more freedom and responsibility as your kids demonstrate their ability to handle the responsibility they've been given. Remember it is much easier to add freedom than to take it away. After setting up the initial boundaries, you can gradually expand or reduce them in response to the good or bad choices made by your child. This teaches kids that their choices have consequences that will affect the quality of their lives. Expanding boundaries is a way for kids who make good choices to earn more freedom and responsibility.

No matter how much we may want to apply a one-size-fits-all formula to setting appropriate boundaries, this is not in our children's best interest. We have to take each child's uniqueness into account and adjust the boundaries to reflect their particular ability to handle responsibility. This will vary from child to child. As we mentioned before, we cannot get caught up in what is "fair" because different children will have different needs.

Try to be specific when setting boundaries. That doesn't mean you have to come up with a huge manual of rules to follow, because no matter how hard you try to write thing everything down, your children *will* find the loopholes. Besides, rigidity isn't the goal. Kids need to learn to adapt to the kinds of individual situations they will face in their lives. But being as clear as possible about what's expected of them helps a lot. They will feel more loved when they know you care enough to set specific boundaries and they see that you will consistently and empathetically deliver consequences when they cross the lines.

Consistency is *so* important. This gives kids a sense of predictability, and as we saw in Emily's case, consistency provides comfort in knowing that certain actions will result in specific consequences. This is not easy, we know. Michelle often shares that every time she saw the wreck our kids had made of their rooms, she would issue new standing orders requiring them to clean up every day. But a few days would pass, she would see their clothes all over the place, and she'd start rationalizing, "Well, maybe their room should be their own special area. Maybe I'm just micromanaging." Eventually, she would relent and let them deal with their space in their own way. A few days later, she would have a bad day and the rules would flip-flop again. Our kids would end up a little confused about the boundaries but confident they could just wait her out—because they learned that her words didn't necessarily mean that a consequence was coming. That kind of waffling didn't create an environment for our kids to learn how to live within the boundaries.

A way to avoid vacillating is to decide in advance the boundaries that are most important to you. It's helpful to realize you have only enough energy to enforce consequences for important issues. Pick your battles. Then make sure you follow through consistently with appropriate consequences on the battles you choose.

One other important point is to resist the urge to sell the "legitimacy" of your boundaries. Parents often get into a debate with their kids over the necessity of a boundary. How many times have you heard your child say, "You're the only mother who isn't letting her kid go"? While it is important to *empathize* with your child's point of view ("You really feel like I'm being unfair"), you really only need to give a brief *explanation* for the boundary ("I don't feel comfortable allowing you to go without an adult"). Going through a long defense of your decision isn't wise. Most likely, your child will see your defensiveness as an invitation to try to persuade you otherwise.

Another key in setting boundaries is to recognize the difference between those that are legitimate and those that are selfish. Setting boundaries selfishly, especially when you're tired, can be tempting, but you cannot set boundaries that serve only your needs. Of course, you can't ignore your needs either. Your goal should be to set up a balanced environment where everyone in the family works and grows together as a team. The boundaries are not to be entirely about you; that would be selfish. Nor can your boundaries be completely selfless, because when you are wearing yourself out sacrificing everything you have for your family, you aren't really helping anyone. Once again, the answer is balance. Balancing the needs of every member of the family, including yourself, is the secret to a happier, more functional family.

We all know parents who are powerhouses of activity. One mother we know has three overachieving kids who have résumés longer than most adults. And Mom has a full schedule of her own. Her typical day starts at 6:00 am and ends around 11:00 pm when she falls into bed exhausted from all the things she has done for her family during the day. Many people admire her for this self-sacrificing lifestyle, but it's difficult to maintain. What initially appears to be selfless sacrifice can eventually damage the parent's health and the well-being of the family as everyone comes to depend on Mom's sacrificial lifestyle.

Running until you drop can also set a negative example for your children. If you feel you have to do everything for everyone, you probably have a difficult time saying no to anyone, and your kids may feel they have to do the same. This can instill a performance-based sense of worth that causes them to believe that their value depends on what they do and can achieve. One daughter of an overextended mom announced, "I've got to sign up for Spanish club because it will help me get into a better college." She was already involved in more activities than a normal girl could reasonably handle, but you can see where she got this notion. Her mother could have modeled better behavior by saying no from time to time and setting more reasonable boundaries on her own activities.

Your kids need to see an example of someone who respects himself or herself enough to say no, especially when others are being disrespectful and crossing boundaries. This provides a model of self-respect they can draw on down the road. One day, somebody will try to persuade your kids to compromise *their* boundaries. (Think alcohol, drugs, sex, or ethics.) When someone treats them with disrespect or pressures them to do something they shouldn't, they are more likely to say no and maintain good boundaries if they've seen it modeled by their parents.

Choosing to remove yourself from an uncomfortable environment can be a valuable example for your children to follow. Imagine your family going to the mall to get school supplies and eat lunch at the food court. That can be fun—something to look forward to. Now imagine that shortly after you get there, one of the kids spots the music store and starts whining about getting a new CD, and another gets mad because you chose the wrong fast food place. Soon everyone's in a bad mood. The "fun" family outing has quickly become a struggle. The dictator is upset because no one is following his directions, the rescuer is upset because everyone is unhappy, and the kids are anxious because they aren't getting what they want.

What should you do in that situation? If you face it as a teaching opportunity, your kids will get a chance to see an example of what it means to respect yourself. First, try giving them a choice by asking, "Would you rather have a good attitude or head home?" If they continue to complain, you can say, "It's sad, but this trip is over. I was looking forward to it. But this isn't fun for any of us, and we're going to have to get up and go home." If only one child has acted up, you might consider taking that child home and going back to the mall with the others, or you could leave him at home with a babysitter the next time.

You could tell him that you'll be happy to have him along when he can demonstrate good behavior in public.

Contrast this approach to a dictator. The dictator typically confronts anxiety by lecturing, nagging, or giving orders. He knows how to have fun at the mall, and he is going to make sure it happens. What happens? The whole scenario turns into a battle for control, and that isn't fun for anyone. The kids react by rebelling or withdrawing, and the teaching opportunity is lost. The focus is no longer on the bad choices the kids have made; it has shifted to the dictator's angry response and the ensuing battle. The consequences are muddled, and the opportunity to send the right message about choices and consequences has been lost.

Let's not forget the rescuers either. Their response to the mall situation is usually to try to lower the anxiety. They will plead with their children to change their minds about what they want, they will whine at everybody to "just stop," or they will rationalize giving their kids what they ask for so everyone can go back to having a good time. While the rescuer is just trying to eliminate the pain, she succeeds only in postponing a learning opportunity, and in modeling that the proper response to anxiety-causing demands is to give in. I doubt any rescuer wants *that* message to be communicated to their kids!

As balanced parents, we must be careful to promote fun in the family but also to exercise the authority God has given us. Those of us who are dictators tend to emphasize authority over fun, and those of us who are rescuers tend to overvalue fun when the exercise of parental authority is called for. A classic example of this rescuing mind-set is when parents of teenagers allow their kids to have alcohol at a party and rationalize, "Well, they're going to drink anyway, so they might as well do it at our house where we can keep tabs on them." The truth is most of those parents are more interested in being seen as their kids' "friend," but by giving in they end up compromising their authority.

A parent's job is to exercise authority and set boundaries. Anticipating that boundaries will not be respected is no excuse for not setting them in the first place, or for not having consequences for violations. In the end, that's confusing for kids. The message they receive is that the rules don't always apply and that it's okay to violate them sometimes. They lose respect for the boundaries *and* for the authorities responsible for setting them. If you ask the kids at one of these parties what they think about the permissive parents, they'll usually describe them as gullible, easy to manipulate, and less deserving of respect.

## LEE'S BOX

I cannot tell you how often teenagers will sit in my office and beg me to ask their parents to hold them accountable. They'll say, "Please don't tell my parents I'm asking for this, but I need them to drug-test me. It's my best hope for staying sober. I want them to give me an excuse to stop using drugs." The first several times I heard this, I almost fell out of my chair in shock. Now I have almost come to expect it. I recognized what they are asking for—real boundaries. They need boundaries to know their parents care about them. Appropriate boundaries make it possible for these kids to have a relationship with their parents. I know that sounds backward, but it is true. Boundaries communicate love. A child must know he is loved. If this is an issue for you, reread Hebrews 12:5–11. Discipline *is* a loving act.

Balancing fun with authority requires a plan. This means earmarking time to relax and enjoy the family without discussing expectations and problems. Michelle and I began to realize that we had a habit of reviewing our kids' lists of responsibilities with them, especially during dinnertime. No sooner had we sat down to eat when our questions began. "Did you do your homework? When is that project due?" and so on. And we were surprised that our boys didn't want to eat with us as a family! But why would they? Dinner with us was no fun at all. It was just one long interrogation, with some meat and vegetables on the side. When you are setting boundaries for your children, also consider putting some boundaries on when you are going to discuss responsibilities and issues, and balance that with quality relational time.

## Bringing It Home

Maybe this chapter about exercising authority and setting boundaries has raised your anxiety level. You know you need to do these things, but for some reason, you find it difficult. You may have to do some soul-searching and take an honest look at your past. If you are a people pleaser, it might be more difficult for you to set boundaries, especially if your kids respond with anger or disrespect. If you were brought up in a dictatorial environment, you might feel like it's your job to rigidly control your children. Pray for wisdom and the insight to uncover any issues from your past that may be influencing your parenting today. If you think you might be blinded to some long-standing patterns, you may want to seek outside help.

If you can balance having fun and exercising authority, however, you'll become much more effective as the central authority in your home. And if you want a new definition of fun, think about the privilege of seeing your kids achieve their potential and grow into their God-given uniqueness. That can happen when you consistently set and enforce good boundaries. The world defines fun in parenting as watching your kids acquire money, beauty, power, and fame. But we believe real joy comes when you watch your kids fulfill God's design for their lives. When I tried to make my son into the baseball player I wanted him to be, it wasn't fun for either of us. When I talk with him about painting, I see his eyes light up and I get to experience a little of his passion as an artist. The right balance gives your kids the freedom to find God's design for their lives and allows you to walk beside them as it happens. That makes parenting fun.

The position of central authority is powerful. It requires wisdom, maturity, and a strong sense of responsibility. Those are the kinds of things that come from God. That's why prayer is vital. God will give His wisdom to those who ask for it. (See James 1:5.) After all, He is the ultimate balancer of truth and love. He calmly gave clear but generous limits in the garden of Eden. He was always present. When His children sinned, He delivered the necessary consequences, but in His love, He met His disobedient children with empathy and covered their shame. He is our model of how to be a calm, loving authority figure even in the face of direct defiance and how to walk alongside our children with empathy despite their poor choices.

# CHAPTER 7

# BACKPACKS AND BOULDERS

## LEE'S BOX

When my daughter was three, I watched her play with a dollhouse that had a latching door. She struggled to get the door open, not realizing she had to turn the handle. I was tempted to reach down and open it for her, being the hero and saving the day, but I resisted the urge. I realized that if I did, I'd spoil her chance to figure it out on her own. Pretty soon she got it open, proudly turned to me, and said, "Look what I did!"

I'm glad I didn't rob her of a three-year-old's victory. We both learned something about her capabilities and that many accomplishments involve some struggle. I try to remind myself of this as she faces new challenges. I want my actions to display that I have confidence in her and respect her enough to let her try.

In the first six chapters, we talked a lot about balance. We looked at the tension between bonding and boundaries, between truth and love, and between having fun and exercising authority. As we looked at the need for balance, you probably noticed your strengths and weaknesses—your natural tendencies as a parent and where you get knocked off balance most easily. The good news is that knowing your weaknesses is the first step to regaining your balance and beginning to change the way you relate to your children.

In this chapter, we turn to another area where balance is essential: knowing when to step in and help a struggling child and when to step back and support the learning process by encouraging him to deal with an issue on his own. When our children struggle with a problem or ask for help, it is difficult *not* to intervene. But it is in their best interest that we learn how to discern when to get involved and how much involvement is enough without being too much. Remember our goal is to help them develop skills they will need as adults.

We know how difficult it is to pull back from jumping in when every fiber in your being screams for you to help! But we encourage you to consider whether intervening may actually be handicapping your kids by making their lives too easy. Think about each situation and ask yourself, "What is the most loving thing I can do, knowing that this situation could be a learning opportunity for my child?" Usually, the answer is to walk alongside your kids as *they* struggle with the problem, offering encouragement and just enough of a boost so they can solve the problem.

Finding the right balance between hands on and hands off may require you to change your parenting philosophy. We talked about it earlier, but it bears repeating. Can you look at the pain of problems and mistakes as an opportunity rather than as something to be avoided? When you recognize that trials can be God's method for your kids to grow and mature, it is much easier to face struggles with a mind-set that asks, *"What* can my child get out of this?" rather than *"How* can my child get out of this?"

You'll recall that God tells us to "consider it pure joy" when we face trials (James 1:2), because He knows struggles are opportunities for perseverance and perseverance leads to maturity. Walking with us through our trials is one of the ways God lovingly helps us become more like His Son. He promises He will never leave or forsake us, and that includes the times we are dealing with adversity. So when our kids face consequences for a poor choice, like violating a boundary, or when they encounter one of the many other challenges kids go through, we might see that God is stretching them and helping them grow and learn to depend on Him.

Most of us turn to God when things are tough. Our struggles are part of God's plan to draw us to Him. When we look at difficult trials from the eternal perspective, it's easier to understand that the trials might be *gifts* from God to develop our kids' character, wisdom, and maturity. If that's the case, isn't it more loving to let them handle the situation and experience the growth than to step in and interrupt God's process? Of course, we know this can be very difficult. When our kids are young, they make small choices and small mistakes, and the consequences are usually minor. But big kids make big choices, and the stakes can be quite high. But as hard as it may be, even with big kids and big choices, we have to learn to look at the situation from the eternal perspective—what they can gain from the struggle—and decide how much involvement is truly best for them.

A mom in one of our classes told a story about her daughter moving from elementary school to middle school. Her daughter was a very good student, but she was really struggling to make the transition from having only one classroom and one teacher each day to having multiple teachers and changing classrooms every class period. Due to this new distraction, she was having difficulty turning in homework and other assignments on time. The mom encouraged her daughter to come up with some ideas that would help her keep up with her new responsibilities. But despite the daughter's concerted effort, a homework assignment got turned in incorrectly and the teacher penalized her severely. The mom was upset and certain the teacher hadn't given her daughter any leeway to compensate for the effort she was making to adjust to the change to middle school. In our parenting class, Mom asked whether we thought she should complain to the teacher or school administration.

What would you say to this mom? We believe the first step is for Mom to look at her motivations for getting involved. If her goal was short-term—to get a better homework grade and relieve the pain her daughter was feeling for the missed assignment—she could have complained to the teacher or administration and tried to fix the problem for her daughter. But would that be the most loving thing she could do for her daughter in the long term? Probably not. Our suggestion was to take the longest possible view of the situation. What if Mom looked at it as if the teacher had presented her and her daughter with a valuable opportunity to talk about real issues that happen every day in a fallen world? Mom knows the world is not always fair and that her daughter will have to learn this important truth. How awesome that the learning opportunity arose when the girl was in fifth grade and had her mom to walk through it with her! In addition, the mom and daughter had a chance to talk about fairness issues when a third party (the teacher), rather than Mom was the "bad guy." That made it easier for the mom to be a true counselor by asking her daughter to brainstorm solutions instead of dictating the daughter's response or trying to rescue her. This situation turned out to be a great example of the difference between treating trials as problems to be avoided versus opportunities to learn.

## Changing Mind-Sets Is a Process—for Everyone

Let's assume you have seen some weaknesses in your parenting style and want to make changes. You approach your children and tell them you want them to make more choices and exercise more responsibility. How do you think they will respond?

Most kids think this is a wonderful idea! More choices and more responsibility sound great *until* the first time they face a consequence for one of their new choices. Then it is likely they will want to return to the old way of doing things. If you've been a rescuer, they will expect you to save them from the consequences. If you've been a dictator, they will want you to give them instructions to follow.

Don't be discouraged! When you make a change in your parenting style, it will take some time for you and your kids to adjust. They are used to the old relationship patterns. Dealing with a rescuer or a dictator may not have been much fun for them, but at least it was predictable. They won't be nearly as excited when they have to start dealing with some of the consequences they will face as a result of your new parenting style. Sometimes, you will need the support of your spouse or other parents to avoid the temptation to revert to your old style.

If your kids are older, this transition period will take longer than with younger kids. Fortunately, it's never too late. We made changes when our boys were sixteen and eighteen. By that point, they had built up a large repertoire of responses from the old days. It seemed they had a Rolodex of scenarios in their heads. If getting really angry had worked to make us rescue or give them a solution, they would get angry to see if it still worked. If anger failed but remorse had been effective before, they tried that out too. They pushed back from a lot of different angles, trying to get us to revert to our old, predictable patterns of behavior.

Part of the reason our kids wanted the "old parents" back is because they had learned how to control us through our old relational style. Even though the old parental responses weren't always fun for them, our boys had spent many years relating to us on those terms. They could predict our behavior and had learned how to navigate it. They knew what to expect under certain situations and that gave them a certain amount of control over our relationship.

## Where to Start?

When you give your kids more choices and more responsibility, where will you begin? Being balanced means you can't allow them to depend on you to run their lives and keep them out of trouble, but it also means you don't want them to be crushed under the weight of too much responsibility. Our suggestion is to teach them responsibility and values through the boundaries you set and the consequences you give. Your boundaries (representing your value system) will provide a foundation and framework for your child to approach problem solving. With each new developmental stage, your child will be challenged to incorporate these boundaries and values into their own decision-making process. Setting good boundaries and giving consistent consequences provides stability so you can support your children, even while you allow them to struggle, grow, and mature.

Before you intervene in one of your children's issues, ask yourself whether jumping in is the most loving thing you can do. If you believe the struggle can teach problem-solving and decision-making skills, encourage your kids with your confidence that they can handle life's difficult situation. To help them mature into self-sufficient adults, resist the urge to solve the problem, and walk beside them empathetically as they learn to solve it for themselves. You can listen as they talk about the problem and let them know you know how difficult or painful the issue is for them while lovingly resisting the urge to take over.

Encourage your kids to come up with solutions on their own. When you do, you communicate confidence and a respect for the fact that they have their own way of handling problems—even if it is different from yours. Remember you've provided guidance through your boundaries and consequences. The challenge for you now is to let go of the results in order to provide room for your kids to learn problem-solving skills and make some mistakes. Let them know you will be happy to brainstorm the solutions with them and tell them you are excited to see what they come up with.

## MICHELLE'S BOX

Not long after Chris and I told our sons we were going to give them more responsibility, Ben had a dentist appointment. He had his driver's license, so I told him his appointment was at nine thirty the next morning and it was his responsibility to get there on time. The next day, when nine fifteen rolled around and he was still in bed, I was so tempted to go in the room and get him up. I paced outside trying to make enough noise to inadvertently wake him, but he slept through it all and woke up after eleven.

"I thought you had a dentist appointment today," I said.

"Oh, gosh, I guess I forgot," he answered. "Will you make me another one?"

I told him he would have to do that himself, and I pointed out that sometimes doctors and dentists charge for missed appointments. That put a new twist on his predicament. Later that day, I heard him on the phone making a new appointment and apologizing for missing the first one. If nothing else, at least it was a great opportunity for him to practice his people skills! He managed to talk his way into another appointment without a fee and made another appointment for nine thirty the next morning. Predictably, the same thing happened. He was still in bed at nine fifteen and I desperately wanted to go in and wake him up. I felt like a negligent mother, but deep in my heart, I knew hands-on experience was what he needed to learn responsibility and accountability.

When Ben finally woke up, he realized he had missed the appointment again. "Do you think they'll charge me for it?" he asked.

"I really don't know," I answered.

As much as I hated for him to pay for a missed appointment, I knew it was his mistake and his responsibility. I told him he would have to work it out with the dentist's office. I heard him on the phone apologizing again, this time pleading with them not to charge him for the missed appointment and promising to be on time for the next one.

He made the next appointment for two thirty in the afternoon so he would be sure to wake up. He was learning something. The day of the appointment, I found something outside the house to occupy my time. He was gone for much of the afternoon, and when he came back home at about four thirty, he looked like he had just won the Nobel Prize.

"I made it to the dentist appointment," he said proudly, brandishing his free toothbrush and floss. It occurred to me this may have been the first time I had allowed him to have complete control over a part of his life, for better or worse. And while I experienced a lot of anxiety letting the dental appointments come and go, if I had stepped in to wake him up or offered to pay for his missed appointments, he would not have learned how to handle this type of situation.

Sometimes, kids learn lessons right away, and sometimes, it takes several attempts. But if we can resist rescuing or solving their problems, they *will* eventually learn. Michelle and I learned the hard way with Bob that this path can be difficult when the consequences are bigger. You may wonder whether your kids really can handle the consequences, and you will be tempted to rationalize why you should jump in, but staying the course and allowing them to struggle will pay off.

Of course, there will be times when you can intervene, but we suggest you give your kids and God a chance to work first, even through the more difficult trials. Like God, you're not going to leave or forsake them, but your goal should always be to be a counselor rather than a rescuer or dictator. After they have struggled for a while, you may ask if they'd like suggestions, but only offer suggestions if they agree. Stay connected; follow up to see how things are going, and keep encouraging them.

## How Much to Carry?

As we said earlier, when we put our kids' problems back in their hands, they often try to get the old parent back. You'll hear things like, "Mommy, I need you," "Just tell me how to do it," or "I can't do this."

These are appeals to the old rescuer or dictator. Your job as central authority is to discern whether they *really* do need you and, if so, how much help they need.

We find helpful advice in Scripture about balancing between hands on and hands off parenting. The Bible is full of parenting wisdom, even when it isn't speaking specifically about parenting. One example is a passage in Paul's letter to the Galatians. Galatians 6:2 tells us to "carry each other's burdens" and in this way "fulfill the law of Christ." That's a great picture of the principle that we should pitch in and help each other as part of being the body of Christ. But three verses later, we're told, "Each one should carry his own load." On the surface, it looks like a contradiction.

If we go back to the original Greek words used for *burden* and *load*, however, we see how this passage defines the balance between helping someone with bigger problems and letting them deal with smaller problems on their own. The word for *burden* in verse 2 is *baros*. It refers to a crushing load. The weight of sin is an example of this kind of burden, and it's a burden we clearly can't carry on our own. So when Scripture tells us to carry each other's burdens, it's referring to the big, heavy issues that are like boulders weighing us down—the things that can crush us and cause lasting harm.

The word for *load* in verse 5 is *phortion*. It refers to a pack like the pack a soldier would carry with him on a day's march. A soldier's pack has loops to go around the arms and is designed for one person to carry by himself. This *isn't* a crushing weight; it refers to something we can carry on our own. So God is telling us there are burdens we should carry together (*baros*) and loads we must carry on our own (*phortion*), and the difference is in each person's ability to handle them. Our job as parents is to determine how heavy the burden or load is and adjust the amount of help we offer based on the child's ability to handle it. The distinction between burdens and loads isn't black and white; it's more like a continuum between offering little or no help on one hand and calling in the cavalry on the other. Negotiating the continuum requires us to really *know* our kids. When we know their personalities, capabilities, and understand where they are developmentally, we will be better equipped to know how much assistance to offer. It's not how heavy the issue is that dictates our involvement but whether or not they have the necessary skills to cope.

We refer to the two ends of the continuum as "backpacks" (the issues a child can carry with only minimal help from parents) and "boulders" (the issues that require us to actively intervene). But no matter where the issue falls on the continuum between backpacks and boulders, our goal is to maximize the learning experience. The experience of confronting the consequences of choices and struggling with possible resolutions is invaluable to our children. This is how God brings them into maturity. Keeping this principle in mind makes it a lot easier to resist the urge to jump in when our kids are dealing with "backpack" issues.

The truth is it can be disrespectful to interpret every problem as a boulder. When we do, we send our children a clear unspoken message: "I don't think you're capable of dealing with this. You need my help." Imagine how deflating that is to a kid trying to grow up. Wouldn't you rather give your kids more opportunities to learn and mature, especially while you are there to counsel with them in the struggle? Kids need to know that you believe in their ability to learn from the process. You know there will be some mistakes and consequences, but you can still encourage your child to try by letting them know that no matter what happens, his or her value to you is never in question. This makes the struggle easier to endure.

Of course, some issues are boulders that our kids aren't developmentally ready to handle. So what should you do with boulders? You might assume the proper response is to take on those issues and fix the problem for your child, but the answer isn't that easy. Instead, the amount of help you offer should depend on your particular child and the extent of the problem. The reason we call the gap between backpacks and boulders a continuum is that in almost every case, a child can contribute *something* to the solution. Even boulder issues can become a learning opportunity for our kids if we are thoughtful about them. This may sound mean-spirited, but the most loving thing we can do for our kids is to offer only the help they need and let them do the lion's share of the problem solving. Not that we don't want to help, but it's more important that we help them develop the confidence and skills to handle life's problems. So how can parents offer assistance and still maximize the learning experience for their kids? The key is scaffolding, a concept we will discuss in depth in the next chapter.

## Bringing It Home

Hopefully by now most of you are ready to make the plunge into being a new parent. You realize it will not be easy and that your kids may not be totally onboard at first, especially when they begin to struggle. They may try to push you back into your old parenting style because they know how to control that parent. But our hope is that the value of teaching long-term life lessons will keep you from reverting to old patterns and that you will begin to see each problem as an opportunity to grow.

Our prayer is also that you will become curious about your kids. This means asking them about their likes and dislikes and using open-ended questions to help you learn what makes them tick. When you do, you will be able to assess each issue they face with an understanding of their personality, perspective, and level of maturity. That will help you evaluate how much help they need to confront the issue and maximize the learning experience. Deciding which problems are backpacks and which are boulders can be done well only when you truly know your kids. And when you do, you will be able to walk alongside them and encourage them as they handle as much of the problem as they can on their own. This can be a tremendous bonding experience for both of you.

# CHAPTER 8

OBEDIENCE

REBELLION

RESPECT

# KIDS NEED SCAFFOLDING

WORLDLINESS

Most issues, whether they are backpacks or boulders, require some amount of help. The question is how much. That's where scaffolding comes in. Our goal is to help our kids just enough so they can learn from and contribute significantly to solving the problem. This is called scaffolding because, like the scaffolding around a building, our objective is to lift our kids up to a position where *they* can successfully solve problems they could not have solved without our help. On a construction site, a scaffold doesn't do any actual labor; it doesn't lay bricks or hammer nails. It just provides the lift the workers need to do those things themselves. When we see our children facing a problem that's too big for them, the most loving way to help is to lift them high enough so they can address it effectively.

Our son Bob attended college in Austin, Texas. Just two weeks after he moved there, his Chevy Tahoe was broken into and everything in it was stolen. This wasn't your average break-in either; they had also tried to steal the car and left behind broken windows, a broken steering column, and a vehicle that wouldn't start. That wasn't all. For some reason, our son's car had become a sort of locker—his books, most of his clothes, and a myriad of other possessions were in the car. The thieves took everything.

He called and asked us what he should do. It was pretty obvious from the tone of his voice that he was frustrated and wanted us to step in and handle the problem. And I'll admit I was very tempted to say, "Let me make some calls and I'll get back to you." But we decided to scaffold him through the situation instead.

First, we suggested that a police report is often needed to file a claim with the insurance company. He wasn't sure how to find the right number for the police so we walked him through some suggestions on where to start. Next, we asked him how he was going to get his car repaired and brainstormed some possible options. Then we gave him the insurance company phone number so he could contact them. Of course, he had never dealt with any of these things, and there were many phone calls back and forth as he tried to hand the problem back to us. We just kept handing it right back—encouraging, empathizing, and scaffolding him along the way.

At one point, he called in frustration to tell me how the insurance company had put him on hold for fifteen minutes and he had finally just hung up. I lamented on how annoying that can be but resisted the urge to cave in and call them myself. Again, I was tempted to step in and "git 'er done," but I resisted for *his* benefit. Eventually, he contacted the police, found a local car repair shop, and completed a long, well-researched inventory of the stolen property with cost estimates for the insurance company. A side benefit for us was when he exclaimed that he had no idea how much money things like books and clothes and cell phones cost! The confidence and maturity he gained from the experience was beyond what we had imagined. Our scaffolding provided the outline of the things he needed to consider—police, repairs, insurance—but he had to do the work.

When we scaffold our kids well, we provide just enough help for them to conquer the problems themselves. There is nothing more empowering and confidence building than to use problem-solving and decision-making skills to handle a difficult situation successfully. Even if we have to give them a big lift, they will understand they have pushed beyond their limitations and expanded their capabilities. In addition, they will be much more invested in seeing the solution through—and more mature after handling it—if we let them manage as much of it as possible.

## LEE'S BOX

As a therapist, my goal isn't to solve my clients' problems but to help them learn to solve problems for themselves. When you think about it, this is a lot like scaffolding. I encourage growth by asking good questions, stimulating thoughts and emotions, and reflecting what I hear. I walk alongside my clients through the process, but it is up to them to do the work. The realizations they come to are much more meaningful because they reach them on their own.

Scaffolding kids involves the same mind-set. As tempting as it might be to intervene and solve your children's problems, that does them a disservice. Instead, look for ways to teach them how to break the problem down into manageable pieces and encourage them to tackle the easiest part first. They are less likely to get overwhelmed and more likely to gain confidence in their abilities.

You may need to facilitate this process by setting shorter deadlines for kids who procrastinate, encouraging them to come up with a schedule of what they are going to do each day to reach a certain goal, or being an empathetic sounding board so they can face and process uncomfortable emotions.

Whether we let our children handle a backpack by themselves or help them conquer a boulder, it is extremely important to be empathetic throughout the process. We want to be able to say, "Wow, that's a tough problem, but I believe you can handle it. I'll help you if you need me, but I bet you can come up with some great ideas. I'd like to hear what you decide, so please let me know what you're thinking." Notice that you aren't volunteering to do the work for them. You're simply making it clear you have confidence they will grow from facing the challenge. If they ask for help, you can give them some ideas to get them started and be available to talk about it along the way. After each suggestion, ask them how they think that might work and give them a chance to think it through. If you need to scaffold, ask the child *how* he thinks you can help. That's part of the learning process too.

Supplying scaffolding for your kids is different for different ages. If a young child wants to pour his own juice, you could provide scaffolding by letting him pour it in the kitchen where there's a tile floor instead of carpeting. And if he spills it, you can give him a towel to wipe it up. The point is you have allowed him to have an experience that he can learn from rather than taking the faster or easier way out and doing it for him. You'll be surprised how pleased a child can be with what seems to you to be the smallest of victories. It's never too early to start. When a child moves past the infant stage, he or she can be given little choices. And your encouraging presence is a source of strength for them as they try new experiences.

You may be thinking, *That's great. It's easy when they're little. But what about scaffolding for big kids? What do you do with a fourteen-year-old struggling with bullies?* That's a great question and it highlights how parenting principles such as scaffolding are applied differently for each child. Like most parents faced with bullying, your knee-jerk reaction may be to do one of two things: urge your child to fight back or take over the problem by talking to teachers, coaches, and even the bully to make sure it doesn't happen again. But let's step back and ask, "What's the best way to scaffold under these circumstances?"

If you ask your child to fight back, you may make the problem worse because you have asked him to do something he probably feels powerless to accomplish. He will be reminded of his weakness and feel even worse because of it. If you jump in and take over the problem, however, you could end up with the same result. The child hears an implied message that you don't think he can handle the bully and is again reminded of his weakness and lack of power.

How can you scaffold the situation? First, try listening. Don't try to solve, blame, or make excuses. Just listen, and ask questions to clarify what you hear. Be very empathetic about the struggle your child is facing. Letting him talk restores some of the power he has lost. After you let him vent, begin scaffolding by asking him what *he* thinks he should do. If he doesn't have any solutions he feels good about, ask if he wants to hear some of yours. If he says yes, give him some ideas, but after each suggestion, ask whether he thinks it will work. You're giving him back some of his power and you're engaging his problem-solving skills. Let him choose, and then ask how he wants you to help. Be careful not to overstep your bounds and take on more than you should. Follow up to see how it turns out for him. Even a difficult situation like this can give you the opportunity for great conversations about living in a fallen world and the grace God provides for His followers.

## The Difference between Scaffolding for Backpacks and Boulders

Knowing the difference between backpacks and boulders is important so you will know how much to scaffold. Here are some thoughts: A backpack issue is something children *can* and *should* handle themselves. *Can* means they are physically and developmentally capable of handling the situation on their own. Try to be very honest in your assessment. Some of us may need to give our kids a little more credit and recognize they may be more capable than we think they are. *Should* means it is not our struggle; it's our child's. We have already discussed at length why we shouldn't take on our child's problems.

In the case of backpacks, we do our best work when we get behind our children and show them we are confident they can deal with the problem. When I'm trying to figure out whether an issue is a backpack or a boulder, I have benefitted greatly by simply asking, "Is this something my son can and should do for himself?"

You'll have to be sensitive about whether you're inclined to make backpacks into boulders. This can be a temptation for rescuers when they see their child in pain and for dictators when their child is not getting the results they expect. Some of us have a tendency to take on our kids' problems because it makes us feel needed or because we want to make sure it gets handled the "right" way. But in every case, we have to ask, "Is this about me or my child? What is his or her greatest learning opportunity in this situation? What is the most loving thing I can do?" We must examine *our* motivations for helping. Are we satisfying a need to control the situation or have our kids reflect well on us, or are we focusing on what will help them grow and mature? Is our paramount concern about their development and ability to be a better problem solver and decision maker? We have to distinguish between meeting our *kids'* needs and meeting *ours*.

Another sure sign that you're dealing with a backpack rather than a boulder is when you feel resentful. If you're constantly rearranging your schedule to take forgotten items to school (in other words, if you're a chronic rescuer) and you're starting to feel resentful about it, you are dealing with a backpack issue. The fact that you are resentful usually indicates you have taken on a backpack that your children should be carrying. Give the problem back to your child to carry.

## MICHELLE'S BOX

We recognize that giving a problem back to your kids can feel mean-spirited, but it's actually a gesture of respect. Think of it this way: when someone micromanages you, you don't feel respect; you feel condescension. One time I went fly-fishing and the guide did almost everything for me. He picked the location, spotted the fish, and held onto my arm as he made the casting motion. When a fish took the bait, he said, "You caught a fish!" But instead of making me feel proud, this just made me angry. He'd caught the fish—using my arm! Instead of feeling elated, I felt patronized. I reflect on that experience when I am tempted to intervene with my boys. While I might be able to prevent a mistake, I might also deprive them of an accomplishment. Giving your children true responsibility means giving them room to succeed or fail and allowing them to deal with the consequences either way.

Respect for your kids is an important consideration when distinguishing between backpacks and boulders. Make sure backpacks remain backpacks and that you're being respectful of your children's responsibilities. Send a clear message that you realize they have the potential to learn how to handle problems.

Let's look at some other examples of backpacks. What should you do with a six-year-old who is learning how to get ready for school in the morning? Which of the tasks should she be taking on? One idea is to start by encouraging her to do one or two things, such as putting on her clothes or brushing her teeth. As she learns to handle the first couple of things, you can add other parts of the morning routine, such as setting her alarm and getting out of bed, deciding if she will make her lunch for school, or having her backpack ready to go. Will she make mistakes? Of course. Your challenge is to be empathetic when she does and to allow her to learn from the consequences.

If you fail to see the value of this process, it's likely you will keep doing your kids' tasks for them long after they are old enough to handle them alone. What happens then? Quite often, *you* will get the blame when homework, a uniform, or a school lunch gets left behind. When that happens, ask yourself whether it is true. Have *you* failed your kids if they get to school without their school project or the supplies they need, or is that an issue your child should have been handling all along? Aren't those the types of backpack issues your kids will have to learn to conquer sooner or later? If your kids don't learn these responsibilities at home where the environment is safe and the stakes are low, they will have to learn them the hard way when the stakes are much higher.

Letting children learn by trial and error can be frustrating and inconvenient. Sometimes, it's downright embarrassing. Our kids' mistakes make it tempting to assume more responsibility than we should, if only to avoid that frustration. When our boys were in high school, Michelle woke them up every morning for school. "Okay, just a minute," they would mumble, and then they fell back asleep. She would go back a little later and warn them they would be late. Sometimes, she even had to yank them out of bed to make sure they made it to school on time. And the next day, it would be the same routine all over again. Sadly, all our kids learned was how to be more effective procrastinators.

It wasn't long before Michelle became resentful at having to drag the boys out of bed. Finally, in frustration, she projected herself into the future. Was she willing to be a personal assistant when our kids had to get up for a college class, go to a job, fill out a credit application, or buy a house? At some point, they had to learn how to do these things on their own. If she kept it up, she would end up being a stumbling block to their growth rather than a positive influence. Eventually, they had to experience the consequences of neglecting responsibilities. She realized that our kids had to be allowed to come face-to-face with the consequences for poor choices like oversleeping and being late so that it would be much more likely that irresponsible habits could be broken. Experience is a great teacher.

Homework is another type of backpack. This is true even though we know many parents who have trouble seeing that the homework is assigned to their children and not to them. Frequently, this problem comes to a head when a child has gotten good test scores but a low homework grade because she forgot to turn in a few assignments. That brings the overall grade-point average down, and for parents who are focused on "success," this can seem like a crisis. Fearing that low grades will derail their child's future can lead to an almost irresistible urge to get on top of the homework situation and make sure the child is always prepared.

## MICHELLE'S BOX

When our son was in sixth grade, he was required to do a "leaf project." The assignment was to collect and build a display for the leaves and seeds of local bushes and trees. The leaf project was well known and a little feared by the parents of sixth-graders at their school. Many of the moms—including myself—took it on themselves to make sure the project went smoothly. Although the assignment was given to the kids, you would find the moms at the local botanical garden, skulking around, gathering samples for our kids' projects. A casual observer might have wondered where the kids were because we were doing all the work. Of course, we rationalized that with all their other activities, it would be more efficient for us to gather the components while the kids were at school.

With all the leaves and seeds collected, it was time to display them in a creative way. By this point, I was way too invested in the project. Although I couched it in the form of "helpful" suggestions, I basically took over the design and execution of the display. In fact, I was a little jealous when I saw the presentation my friend had created for her son! I also remember being disappointed when my son finally received "his" grade on the project: B+.

What happens when a parent gets too involved in homework assignments? The child is deprived of one of the best learning opportunities his school can provide. If you think about it, homework is one of those tasks that has a wide application to real life. It augments the classroom learning process, of course, but it also teaches responsibility, time management, teamwork, and delayed gratification. Homework teaches our kids how to tackle a challenge from start to finish. The skills they learn from doing homework will prepare them for the job they will have one day.

Rather than dictating the homework process, try offering a little scaffolding first. Kids who are starting to receive homework may need some help establishing a routine. Encourage your child to consider where, when, and how she studies best. Be respectful of her personal preferences rather than trying to fit her into your mold. For instance, some kids do better with a little music playing in the background. Some kids like to study at a desk while others prefer the bed or a chair. Is she able to concentrate better if she's eaten a snack? Are there any supplies that would be helpful, such as a special binder, planner, or pens? Some kids like to finish all their homework in a marathon session, while other kids like to take a break every thirty minutes. You can even be a good example for your child by working on *your* homework (maybe some work you brought home or a devotional) at the same time your child is working on hers. Let her learn by doing the work and facing the challenges that arise. Only give assistance if she asks for it, and then just enough to get her back on track.

If you have taken on too much responsibility for your child's homework and have decided to hand it back, it is helpful to let the teacher know what you're doing. Explain that it may look like you aren't staying on top of your child's homework but that you're trying to instill a new sense of responsibility. Most teachers will appreciate what you're trying to do and cooperate with the process.

## Boulders

Now let's look at the kinds of issues we find on the boulder end of the continuum. These are issues that require the parent to take a more active role on behalf of the child—at least initially. A physical injury can be an example of a boulder. Usually parents have to make immediate decisions on behalf of an injured child, such as getting to the doctor, filling prescriptions, and filing insurance claims. Other examples of boulders include breakups with boyfriends or girlfriends, divorce, and even death. In some of these cases, a parent might even need to seek professional counseling for their child.

While we can't always prevent boulder issues, we can support our kids so they can work through the problems without being crushed. The goal is to provide enough resources so they can handle as much of the issue as possible and begin to develop the skills necessary to handle other difficult issues in the future. Regardless of the boulder issue, look for ways for your child to participate in the solution. For example, with an injury, a parent can encourage the child to take an active role in her recovery. Maybe she could call a friend to help her carry her books to class or brainstorm ways to make crutches more comfortable. Older kids can schedule their own rehab appointments or doctor visits. With mental health issues, such as depression or anxiety, the parent could give the child a choice of therapists and coordinate with the therapist to maximize the child's coping resources.

## Developmental Boulders

A backpack can turn into a boulder when our kids don't possess the skills required to handle some of the tasks they are given. It is important to have realistic expectations about our children's capacity to actually do some of the things they are asked to do. The next chapter covers the developmental stages of children to help parents understand what skills they should expect from their kids at various ages.

You may have noticed some situations where your child tends to overreact and lash out in frustration. For younger kids, this may be a tantrum. For older kids, it may be explosive outbursts of anger or completely shutting down and withdrawing. What looks like disobedient or stubborn behavior might just be your children's way of responding when they don't possess the skills for a task they've been given. When this happens, giving them consequences will just add to their frustration. So what can you do when your children struggle with a skill that is beyond their developmental capabilities? One option is to model the skill they will acquire later. These skills might include helping them verbalize their concerns and feelings, identify the problems to be solved, consider possible solutions, and weigh the likely outcomes of these solutions. For example, young children can get frustrated because they do not have the language skills to communicate clearly. You can provide words to help them identify and express their feelings. For example, "You sure are angry that I'm changing your diaper" or "You are frustrated your sister took your toy." As the child listens to you identifying feelings and talking through potential solutions, he learns how to think in a more organized and less impulsive way.

Provide opportunities for your child to learn and practice new skills, such as transitioning from one activity to another (e.g., from play to dinner or from TV to homework), taking no for an answer, or expressing thoughts and feelings in a respectful way. Skills training is a great way for your child to understand the skill you are trying to teach, rehearse it under less stressful circumstances, and practice applying it to the kinds of problems that are causing frustration. We recommend that parents come up with creative ways to introduce kids to new skills and allow them to practice in a relaxed atmosphere. Rather than trying to tackle the entire task all at once, divide it up into bite-size pieces so they can gain a sense of accomplishment as they conquer each piece. Several books provide excellent examples on how to teach these skills effectively. We recommend *No More Meltdowns,* by Jed Baker, and *Treating Explosive Kids,* by Ross Greene and Stuart Ablon.

Some skills will require professional help. Many counselors offer social skills training in groups with other children of the same age for kids who are having trouble adjusting socially. But no matter how you train your kids, keep in mind that while you provide opportunities to acquire skills, it is necessary for your child to own the challenge of actually learning and applying them. No matter where your child falls on the skills spectrum, resist the temptation to fix the problems yourself. Learn to scaffold them through the struggle.

## Fix-It Mode versus Be-There Mode

Whether your child is dealing with a backpack or a boulder, it is always a good idea to ask yourself, "Am I in a fix-it mode or a be-there mode?" When our kids are struggling, it raises our anxiety level and makes us want to stop the pain as quickly as possible—both for them and for us. As a result, we may try to "fix" whatever is wrong by offering unsolicited suggestions or taking curative steps without consulting them. Although we are motivated by love, this often just ends up adding to their pain. The result is a child who doesn't feel understood, who may try to justify his or her right to be in pain, and who will be less likely to share important issues with you in the future.

Boulders may require a certain amount of parental involvement at least initially, but if we overdo it, we miss important opportunities to make our children feel known and understood. What kids usually crave is not someone to charge in and fix the problem but someone who will listen and empathize with their situations. Instead of spending your energy fixing the problem, use it to listen carefully to your children as they pour their hearts out. Take time to reflect what you hear them saying about their feelings. Reflective listening gives your kids a chance to correct any false conclusions you might have made, and more importantly, it communicates that you truly care how they see the situation—that you are not just interested in getting the problem solved or giving advice. What a profound way to "weep with those who weep" (Rom. 12:15). Only after you've invested the time listening should you ask how they plan to handle the situation or if they'd like to hear some suggestions.

Here's an example: Your child comes home from school crying because other kids have excluded her from their clique. With respect to her peers, she is likely feeling unpopular, insecure, and embarrassed—powerful emotions. This is a big deal to a child trying to form relationships outside her family. Your fix-it mode may include inviting all the cool kids over for a party, reassuring your daughter that she can find better friends, or trying to convince her that the so-called cool kids really aren't very cool to begin with. But your actions are probably just going to add to your daughter's distress. The be-there mode, on the other hand, lets your daughter talk about the situation for as long as she needs to and tries to understand the emotions she is feeling. Great be-there statements include "Wow, that must have hurt" and "You really felt left out! What was that like for you?" Statements like these communicate that you are genuinely trying to see the situation from her perspective. They also let her know you can handle strong emotions without taking over a problem that is rightly hers.

When you stay in the be-there mode, it frees up your kids to solve problems on their own. You can help them with questions like "What do you think you're going to do?" and "What ideas do you have?" Give them a real chance to think about potential solutions. Before offering your thoughts, ask if they'd like to hear some ideas. Then, instead of pushing your suggestions on them, ask how they think each potential solution might work. Talking things out and brainstorming this way is empowering. This puts the situation in the hands of the children and frees them up to deal with it in their own ways.

If you think about it, this is how all meaningful relationships work. Imagine telling a friend about one of your issues and then having to listen to him or her tell you what you did wrong and what you should do next. No one enjoys that, and we can't blame our kids if they don't want to relate to us that way. We all gravitate toward people who listen to and "get" us, and it's no different for our kids. In most cases, we don't even have to fix the problem; we just need to listen and offer encouragement and love.

## MICHELLE'S BOX

I learned how important it is to respect your kids' space when Ben was away at college. Chris and I visited him several months into the semester, and frankly, I was horrified when I saw his apartment. His mattress was on the floor and he had no sheets or pillow, even though he had the money to buy them. When he said he hadn't gotten around to buying them, I assumed the role of rescuer. I told him we were going to the store to get him fixed up. He seemed a little reluctant, but I was on a mission. As we went up and down the store aisles, I saw lots of things I thought he needed, but when I asked him, he kept saying, "Well, if I do, I'll come back and get it later." But I would insist on getting it, assuming I was being a tremendous help. I was in my element.

When we finished shopping, I got busy setting everything up in his apartment. I was excited and expected him to be just as excited too. But that wasn't the response I got. He wasn't rude; he just wasn't responding as enthusiastically as I thought he should. Finally, I said, "I kind of feel like you might be happier if we took all of this back."

I'll never forget his response. "I can see how you might feel that way. I appreciate all this stuff and there is no doubt I would be much more comfortable. But I've spent a lot of my life dependent upon having material things, and I don't want to get back in a place where I need a lot of things to be happy."

I realized I had never stopped to ask what *he* wanted. Instead, I set up his apartment the way I would have wanted it, thinking anything I did would be a welcome improvement. But he needed time to process and decide what would work best for him. I apologized for assuming I knew what he wanted and commended him on his mature attitude about possessions.

We have talked to a number of parents who struggle with issues much more grave than those we've discussed above. It is heartrending to let your kids struggle with big issues, but we also know far too many kids who are still challenging the boundaries and failing to learn hard lessons because their parents keep rescuing them from the consequences of bad choices.

Let's walk through an example based on a situation we have seen too often. Imagine your eighteen-year-old son calls from jail. He has been arrested for suspicion of driving under the influence of drugs or alcohol. He has been in the jail for four or five hours before he makes his phone call. He is scared, tired, sick, and really wants out. What do you do?

What many parents almost automatically do is call a friendly lawyer and ask him to help get the boy out. That's expensive, of course, so the parents give the lawyer a big check for his fees, the bond, court costs, and so on. Then Dad drives to the jail and picks up his son. Dad is angry, scared, confused, and upset that his night's sleep ended with an early morning trip to the jail. On the way home, he vents his frustration for the inconvenience, expense, and embarrassment this crisis will cause for the family if it becomes public. The son, used to being rescued and to the lectures that follow, promises that this was the first time and he will never do it again. He also promises to pay the money back to Dad.

Dad wants to believe this is an isolated incident, so he clings to the son's words and promises to hold him responsible for the money. The son, sensing some buy-in from Dad, describes all the other things going on that night and how a number of friends got away with much more. He hints it might have been someone else's fault that he had alcohol or drugs in his system. Then he tells his dad about the arrest, the jail time, and how unfair it all was. The father starts to get a little angry and subconsciously sees an opportunity to blame someone else for his pain. He thinks, *Nobody treats my boy that way,* and he is soon off to get the charges dropped and to make somebody in the justice system pay. Meanwhile, the son knows he has knocked his dad completely off balance, that he has taken control of the situation, and that everything will be back to normal if he just plays his cards right for a couple of days. In fact, there's a good chance he won't end up paying for the lawyer or the court fees. And if Dad has enough money and clout, he may not suffer any consequences at all. Sound familiar?

Now let's look at this situation from another perspective and see if there are better alternatives. When the son called from the jail, what could Mom or Dad have done differently? One idea would be to let the experience teach a hard lesson by leaving him in the jail until morning, or later if Mom and Dad have something else they had to do. Leaving him in jail may be *more* loving then bailing him out because it has a better chance of teaching him tough lessons. The parents have to ask themselves, "Whose choices landed him in jail? Do I trust God to use these circumstances to sanctify my son? What can he learn from this situation that he is not learning in our home?" The answers, while painful, are also obvious. Jail time has a way of breaking through to even the most entitled kids.

When the parent finally does go down to the jail, what's the next step? He could have a lawyer in tow with the fees already paid, but that may not be the best way to teach a significant life lesson. Think about scaffolding. How could you scaffold the situation instead of taking it over? How about helping him look through the yellow pages to find a lawyer and then letting him make the phone call himself? That is humbling and a great lesson for a kid used to having everything done for him. He will also have to negotiate a way to pay the fee, which opens up a whole range of other possibilities for parents to teach important lessons about borrowing money, collateral, interest, payment terms, and so on. Then he will have to meet with the lawyer and make some decisions about how the case will handled. As a parent, you can be there with him counseling, encouraging, and offering suggestions, without giving the impression this situation is your responsibility. As the case proceeds through the system, you can allow the boy to be responsible at every stage.

You may think you could never let this happen because the consequences are too great. The boy could lose his chance at college, scholarships, or a good job. He may even have to do some time in jail. You may be so worried that you are willing to forego the learning opportunity to ensure his future doesn't get derailed. But these kinds of decisions have consequences for you as well. A proverb says if you rescue a fool, you will have to do it again. (See Prov. 19:19.) The likelihood is that you will only have postponed the learning process until the next incident. Even worse, you may have taught your son a very different lesson—that there are no significant consequences when he makes really poor choices.

When the potential consequences are great, the actual consequences need to be especially significant. While the boy may have avoided seriously injuring himself or others this time, that might not be the case the next time. Letting the consequences run their course can be embarrassing and painful for parents, but as Christians, we know God can take any situation and turn it into good for those who love Him. (See Rom. 8:28.) Can you trust Him with a situation like this? The fact is *only* He can be trusted. You may choose to cosign a loan or help choose the lawyer, but you will be doing your son a big favor if you let him work through each problem first, offering only enough help that he can start solving his problems for himself.

Many parents reading this may struggle with tough issues like teen pregnancy, criminal behavior, eviction, or substance abuse. You may have done your best to intervene on your child's behalf only to find him or her continuing to make the same poor choices. We've been there. Walking through the journey of our son's drug problems required an incredible amount of soul-searching. No matter how much we loved Bob, we couldn't control whether he would ultimately decide to change. It was a challenge to know when our efforts to provide support were helpful and when they were enabling the problem. Because we loved him, it was hard to be objective, but eventually we knew we had to give him the hard choice to either enter a long-term rehabilitation program or face criminal charges and possibly go to prison. That choice and an assurance of our love were all the scaffolding we had to offer.

Few situations in life challenge our trust and faith in God as releasing our children to Him when they are engaged in harmful behavior. Letting go and allowing them to suffer the consequences does not mean we are forsaking them. On the contrary, it can be the most unselfish thing we can do. This may require tough boundaries, such as physically separating yourself from them for a time. It may be that all you can offer is an assurance that no matter what choices they make, you will always love them and pray for them.

Two and a half years after giving Bob that gut-wrenching choice, he wrote me a letter for Father's Day. With Bob's permission, I would like to share a portion of it with you.

*Dad,*

*I wanted to write something to say how much I love and appreciate you … I don't know where I would be without you … The change that came when you realized your life was not your own but God's has had the biggest impact … Having the guts to cut me off led me to eternal life! That decision was the catalyst to bringing me to REAL faith in Christ. Maybe I am your first disciple. I love the conversations and time that we have now to work out the call of God on our lives and how it's confusing and hard, but right and most important. Thank you for loving me so much even when I was against you. I am so thankful for who you are and all you've done.*

*Love, Bob*

## Bringing It Home

As we presented the concept of backpacks and boulders to live audiences, we realized it is not as important to distinguish between the two as it is to understand how much help we should provide to maximize the learning experience for a child. We don't want to interfere with a lesson God is using to make our kids more mature. When we recognize an issue as being on the backpack end of the continuum, we should be careful to offer more encouragement than suggestions. When we see an issue on the boulder side, we should be careful to think it through and try not to take over the issue but to look for ways the child can be involved in the problem solving and implementation of the solution. It takes practice, and you won't get it right every time. But being empathetic and walking alongside your kids gives you the chance to discern how much help they need.

Talking through a situation with other parents who are familiar with these principles can be helpful too. Being objective with your kids can be hard. An outside perspective can usually help clarify things. We see this a lot in our classes. Parents have great advice for each other but have difficulty seeing the issues in their own families. Being a good parent sometimes requires the humility to ask honest questions and seek input from others who can help us see whether we are parenting with pure motives.

# CHAPTER 9

OBEDIENCE

REBELLION

RESPECT

WORLDLINESS

# HOW DO KIDS GROW AND MATURE?

During the course of teaching parenting classes, we often hear parents express similar concerns, such as "Yikes! My four-year-old is lying!" "How come my seven-year-old asks why fifty times a day?" or "Should I be worried that my son has an imaginary friend?" I can remember one distraught mother who approached us in tears. Until recently, her fourteen-year-old son had enjoyed spending time with her and had frequently asked for advice about things like friends and school. But she noticed that over the last few months, he was pulling away from her. He seemed more interested in hanging out with his friends and confiding in them. She missed how close they had been and wondered if she had done something to push him away. We told her that she was likely seeing the same developmental path that millions of moms before her had seen. Although she took it personally, her son was just going through an expected and necessary stage.

Watching a tiny baby become an adult over the course of a couple of decades is an amazing experience. As they grow, God uses a series of fascinating developmental stages that gradually build on each other and move children toward maturity.

This complex process requires a lot of patience and love from parents, however. Knowing where a child is on the developmental pathway can help parents be more empathetic and better understand the behavior they see in their kids. Far too often, we hear parents ascribing adult motives to kids' behavior. That can lead to difficulties in relationships. Some parents make the children's behavior a personal issue when it is really a developmental one.

How does understanding a child's developmental stages reduce anger and enable parents to demonstrate more empathy for our kids? When we understand these stages and the unique behaviors that accompany them, we are more likely to have age-appropriate expectations. Some of the things they do can appear manipulative or irrational if we don't understand what developmental challenges they're walking through. But if we recognize which behaviors are normal for their developmental stage, we can maintain realistic expectations, avoid construing their actions as personal attacks, and give consequences with much more empathy.

Studying our kids' developmental stages also helps parents better understand the struggles their kids are facing. When we are willing to see the world through their eyes, we can express empathy much more easily and effectively. Understanding where they are intellectually, relationally, and morally prepares us to walk with them through the developmental process in a more supportive way.

It is also important to understand these stages when we're trying to provide scaffolding for our kids. In order to help them reach higher without doing all the work for them, we have to know where they are in their development and the kinds of issues they are facing at that particular time in their growth. Knowing how they are maturing helps us scaffold them appropriately.

## Four Stages of Development

We divide the child development process into four general stages, based on research in the field of human growth.

- the infant/toddler stage (from birth to two years)
- the preschool stage (from three to six years)
- the elementary stage (from six to twelve years)

- the teenage stage (from twelve to nineteen years and beyond)

These stages are somewhat arbitrary, and they certainly aren't distinct, separate phases with clearly defined boundaries. Every child moves through these stages at a different pace. Those who go through them quickly aren't necessarily super talented, and those who go through them slowly aren't always developmentally challenged. And as they try to move from stage to stage, they may vacillate back and forth for a while before clearly growing into the next stage. These four divisions are simply general guidelines for the developmental process.

Within each of these stages, we'll look at child development from three perspectives: relationally, intellectually, and morally. While their initial relationships will be centered on the family, those relationships will expand in a lot of different directions as they grow and interact more and more outside the home. We will look at how these relationships evolve and become more complicated. When considering their intellectual development, we'll look at what they know and how they process information into knowledge. Morally, we will be examining how they define and learn the difference between right and wrong. Because we tend to look at our children through adult eyes, we often have adult expectations for them. Understanding each of these elements will help us avoid misplaced expectations and relate to our kids in age-appropriate ways.

The developmental stages are a progression. Initially, a child learns how to balance bonding and boundaries within his family, then with nonfamily individuals, and then with groups. The eventual goal is to help them learn how to maintain close relationships while embracing the unique individual God created them to be. Our model for the perfect balance between bonding and boundaries is the Trinity—three distinct persons but one individual essence. We know our kids won't reach perfection, but that's the goal—to find the balance that God models for us in the relationships of the Father, Son, and Spirit. To achieve that balance, God's developmental process emphasizes different goals for each stage. Some stages are more concerned with bonding and others with boundaries, and some stages are focused on interacting with individuals while others are concerned with understanding groups of people.

The biological, social, intellectual, and spiritual aspects of a child's development also advance along the stages with a sort of supernatural scaffolding. God lifts His kids up just high enough that they can conquer the demands of each stage, and as they progress, He prepares them for the challenges of the next stage. He starts by introducing them to simple bonding within the family. Then He gives them the chance to experience simple boundaries with family and a few close friends. Next, they learn about bonding and boundaries with people outside the family, many of whom are new and different kinds of authorities. Finally, He leads them into complicated relationships, balancing bonding and boundaries with many groups and individuals and getting them ready to start the whole process over with their own family.

## The Infant/Toddler Stage

Relationally, the infant/toddler stage is all about bonding with a caregiver. A small baby can see only about eighteen inches—the distance between a nursing baby's head and his or her mother's face. The main goal of this stage is for the baby to become securely attached to a caregiver. A baby is not capable of manipulation or deceit. When they cry, it is because they have a real need and the only way they know to get the need met is to cry.

A baby's intellectual capacity is limited to simple cause and effect, based on pleasure and pain. If something causes pleasure, they repeat it; if it causes pain, they avoid it. Interestingly, because babies are concerned almost entirely with bonding at this stage, they become so bonded to their caregivers that they see everything the caregivers do as something *they* caused.[10] For example, if a baby cries because he is hungry and Mom feeds him, he understands only that *he* cried and got fed. He doesn't see Mom as a separate person; she is only an extension of him.

Moral development also is shaped by pleasure and pain during this stage. If something is pleasurable, it's good. If it causes pain, it's bad. The response of a parent—whether it is anger or encouragement—will reinforce what the child believes about right and wrong. It is especially important for parents to understand that getting angry or withdrawing affection at this stage is likely to cause the infant to respond with confusion and fear. The only way he knows how to communicate his needs is through crying. If crying sometimes brings relief but other times brings anger and pain, he will not understand the difference between the two parental responses. This puts him in an impossible position and hinders secure attachment.

## LEE'S BOX

I see so many kids in my office who struggle to feel connected to their parents—especially their fathers. A lack of attachment can make kids feel anxious and fearful because they don't feel safe or accepted for who they really are. The long-term effect of poor attachment is that these kids find it difficult to attach to *their* kids when they become parents. The cycle repeats itself.

Attachment is critical for all relationships. Secure attachment gives children the sense that they are unconditionally loved and frees them up to take on the world knowing they can always find comfort and support at home. Becoming securely attached to your kids will require one-on-one time with them, listening to their thoughts and ideas, and asking good, open-ended questions. Empathy is the key. You need to be willing to get down on the kids' level and see the world through their eyes. This is more difficult if you didn't have the benefit of secure attachment with your parent. If this is the case, it may be helpful to seek counseling to better prepare you to provide secure attachment for your kids.

As a child approaches each successive stage, he will become more and more sophisticated and it will be difficult to tell when he actually makes the transition to the next stage. That's perfectly all right and even expected. As the toddler progresses toward the preschool stage, for example, he will find himself puzzled by the fact that "others" are now in his life, such as Mom and Dad. He will have more coordination, mobility, words, and gestures as he matures, and he will entertain more complicated ideas of right and wrong. He is primed to move on to the next stage.

## The Preschool Stage

When kids transition from the infant/toddler stage to the preschooler stage, their relational development takes on a different agenda. They have learned a lot about bonding, and now they can begin to run some experiments on boundaries. They are beginning to realize the world contains others, that it is not just them. Also, these kids begin to realize that these others have an effect on their pleasure and pain. They start to understand that Mom and Dad are distinct from them, and they begin to explore that distinction. One of the ways they establish their first boundaries is with the word *no*. This can be their favorite word when they run early experiments in boundaries. They are like little scientists, but they're not very skilled yet. They may even say no to things they want as they run their first simple boundary experiments.

Michelle and I saw this when Lee's then three-year-old daughter opened some cabinet doors, stuck her head inside, and shouted, "No, no, no!" We finally asked what was going on. Lee answered, "Oh, she knows she shouldn't say no to us, so she says it into the cabinet because she *really* wants to say it." That's a perfect example of how the need to exercise independence is wired into children during this stage. "No" is a typical way to try it out.

Intellectually, kids at this stage are concrete thinkers. They tend to focus on just one thought or concept at a time and learn from what they can touch, feel, and do themselves. They are not yet able to think abstractly or hypothetically. What does this mean? They will need things explained to them in simple terms. You'll lose them if you expect them to follow shifts in the conversation or draw their own conclusions. For example, let's say a four-year-old is taking toys away from her two-year-old brother. She will have trouble if her mother says, "Why are you taking away his toys? How would that make you feel?" The mom is asking the child to put herself in the little brother's shoes—something that requires abstract thinking. (Although children are able to acquire a few basic elements of abstract thinking during childhood, the real ability to think abstractly doesn't occur until about age ten, and it requires years of practice to fully develop.)[11] It would be much clearer for the mom to set clear parameters and give her daughter two choices on how to respond. For example, "If you take your brother's toys away, you will not get to keep on playing. Would you rather play with your toys (as opposed to her brother's) or watch television?"[12]

Moral development in this stage is still shaped by pleasure and pain. But this becomes more complicated because they are now aware of other people as being separate from them. They slowly start to expand their concept of right and wrong to include how the actions of others affect them and vice versa.

When kids at this stage begin to exercise independence for the first time, they are bound to make mistakes, and they will need to have consequences. They will break things, make inappropriate comments, and behave poorly as they try to be unique individuals. The resulting discipline they earn may feel to them as if the bond to their parent is being jeopardized. While they really want to be independent, they want to feel safely attached to their parent as well. So a common way kids in this stage try to preserve the bond when they cross a boundary is to lie. Many parents become concerned when this happens and worry their child will grow up to be a pathological liar. It helps when parents see the developmental roots to this behavior. It is necessary for their kids to exert independence, but they will sometimes go too far. Anticipating the threat that discipline appears to have on their bond with their parents often motivates kids to lie in order to avoid the discipline. When parents understand this, they are more likely to empathize with the dilemma the child is facing. As they deliver consequences, they can assure the child that he is unconditionally loved while explaining that lying is not an acceptable way to avoid consequences for poor choices. Out of love, they deliver consequences for lying, but they do it empathetically because they understand the developmental struggle their child is facing.

Kids at this stage sometimes create an imaginary friend to help resolve the tension between bonding and independence. This "friend" can walk with them through the scary things they are dealing with as they become more independent. The son of one of our friends had an imaginary friend named John, and every time our friend's son stepped too far outside his boundaries, he would blame it on John. In his imaginary world, the son made all the right choices and John got blamed for all the bad ones. He wanted to watch and see the consequences when John made a bad choice, without risking his bonding. That makes perfect sense from a developmental perspective; the child believes he can maintain the bond with his parents while still exploring new territory.

## The Elementary Stage

In the elementary stage (ages six to twelve), the relational challenge increases substantially with the dramatic increase of other people in our children's lives. These kids have started school. They are playing sports, going to dance classes, taking music lessons, and spending more time with friends. They have a lot more people in their lives! In the previous stages, they learned bonding and boundaries in the context of family and close friends, but their world has rapidly expanded. God has prepared them to take what they learned in the prior stages and apply it to an ever-widening number of people and situations.

Intellectually, their brains are primed for input and they ask a lot of why questions. They are being confronted with an influx of new information through school and outside activities, and God has specifically equipped their brains to start processing this increased load. They become information gatherers. They become interested in family, who they are, where they came from, and who and what they will be when they grow up. They want to know more about themselves and about their world. They will ask why until you just can't answer anymore. It is important to remember, however, that they are still concrete thinkers who have not yet developed the ability to think in abstract or hypothetical ways.

Socially, these kids are learning about relational dynamics outside the family for the first time. Because of their concrete thinking, they will likely gravitate and bond to others based on a single, common characteristic, such as being the same gender or interest in a particular type of toy or activity. This is why kids in this stage often narrow their focus to "girls only" or "boys only" clubs, or hang out with kids who collect the same baseball cards or some other common interest. They are harmonizing bonding and boundaries with a number of new people, and it helps to practice doing that with only one concept at a time.

In the moral part of this stage, kids are finally growing out of the pleasure/pain principle for determining right and wrong. They realize there are many other people in the world, and life isn't just about their pleasure and pain. They have to learn how to negotiate bonding and boundaries with all these other people. They know they can't base their actions on what feels good to them. For example, it might feel good to hit another kid and take his toy, but the adults around him will discipline him for doing that. They begin to look for a new way to determine what is right and wrong. They usually end up adopting a rules-based morality based on the concept of "fairness." Fairness often replaces the pleasure/pain principle and becomes the highest principle for kids in this stage.

From a developmental standpoint, it is understandable that kids would adopt strict rules for interacting with others. Because they don't have the ability to think abstractly, they aren't capable of applying different principles to different situations. They gravitate toward hard-and-fast rules because, in most cases, rules are easy to follow and it is easier to know when the rules have been broken. You can tell when a child is in the pleasure/pain mode because he will be willing to endure significant pain in order to do what's "fair." He will insist that you be fair as well. This gives you an opportunity to explain that fairness is not the highest principle. You can tell him that you base your choices on what is best for each child rather than on what is "fair."

You might guess that this is the developmental stage at which the Pharisees seem to have gotten stuck. They were very big on moral codes and rules and defining right and wrong down to the minutest details. While Jesus summarized God's law in two overarching commandments—love God and love your neighbor—the Pharisees felt it necessary to decide how the commandments should be applied in every possible situation. They had lots of rules, and people were either in or out of their group based on their ability to keep these rules. That's a lot like kids in the elementary stage of development. This is a necessary stage of maturity, but it is not the final stage. Mature people learn to move beyond rules to principles.

## The Teenage Stage

As kids enter the teenage years, they enter a new stage of development, but interestingly, this stage has a lot of similarities to the toddler stage. In the teenage stage, kids will turn up the heat in testing boundaries but will still want to make sure they are bonded to Mom and Dad. Of course, a difference between these two stages is that the challenges are bigger because the kids are bigger, but the basic questions are the same. "Where are the boundaries?" "What happens when …?" "Am I still okay with Mom and Dad if I …?" The major difference is that teenagers are aware they are moving into a new, independent phase of their lives and that they must negotiate bonding and boundaries with many people outside the family. This raises their anxiety and is a partial explanation for why teens can be anxious and irritable.

God's plan is for kids eventually to leave Mom and Dad and form a family of their own. For teens to move to the adult stage, however, they must face some challenges. It is during this stage that they become capable of thinking abstractly and hypothetically. They will begin to adopt principles and values rather than rules to negotiate bonding and boundaries with others. They must start putting the pieces together to form a worldview of their own. It sounds complicated (and it is), but thankfully you will be able to walk through this stage with your kids as their counselor. Most parents fear the teenage years, but a little understanding will help you overcome your fear and look forward to being able to relate to your kids on a deeper relational, intellectual, and moral level. Knowing how they are designed will help when your kids do some of the weird, quirky things kids do when they are in this stage.

Efforts at close bonding with another teenager are very common in the early part of the stage. Kids need to learn to bond closely with someone outside the family, and they won't be very good at it at first. In some cases they will become so bonded they will seem to lose their own identity within the other person. Sometimes, this plays out with a best friend. It can also be seen in those really intense romantic "puppy love" relationships. You'll hear, "That's not what Bobby says. *He* says it should be this way." In many cases, what appeared to your teenager to be a deep connection will prove to be superficial, and he or she will be hurt when the relationship ends. The best, most loving thing you can do is be a good listener and set a great example. Kids in this stage need your encouragement as they practice bonding.

From ages fifteen to nineteen, the focus of bonding will also include groups of people, such as a team or club. Kids will run their experiments on bonding and boundaries in the context of groups as well as individuals to help them see how relationships work on a larger scale. At first they may be inclined to an all-or-nothing approach, being very loyal to the group and bonding to the point where it seems as if they are sacrificing their individual identity for that of the group. But as they mature and learn how to negotiate different levels of relationships, they will realize they can have differing opinions and still be bonded. A teenager will learn he need not agree on everything or with everyone in the group, yet he can still be a valuable part of the group. These kids will be able to move past the single-minded thinking of the elementary stage and enjoy different levels of bonding and boundaries. That's one of the goals in this stage—to see our kids bond with other individuals and groups while maintaining their own individuality. One tip: when your kids try on a new group's identity, they may seem more loyal to the group than to their immediate family. Don't take their actions personally. It's just a stage.

## MICHELLE'S BOX

It was difficult for me when our boys stopped talking to me and wouldn't tell me what was going on in their lives. I thought it was because they were mad at me, punishing me for some slight, or not trusting me anymore. In fact, they were learning how to have close relationships outside the family. In the process, they distanced themselves from me. They weren't trying to hurt me, but they didn't know any other way to begin the process of "leaving and cleaving." In their loyalty to friends, they weren't ready to share everything with me. They were still working out the rules of trust and disclosure, and they were erring on the side of the new group, not wanting to offend their new friends. At the time, it seemed as if they valued their friends more than me, but it wasn't personal. It was a part of the normal developmental process. Learning to be loyal to people outside the family is a part of growing up.

### It's Not Personal

Understanding the tendency for parents to take things personally is one reason parents should be aware of the developmental stages. Looking at your kids' behavior through the lens of human growth can change your perspective considerably. What looks like manipulation at one stage probably wasn't intended to be personal. When your teenagers are loyal to a group, it doesn't necessarily mean they aren't loyal to you as a parent. They are simply working out one of the challenges they need to master at that point in their development.

The intellectual development taking place during the teenage stage is profound. After all, this is the last stage before they become adults and have to function on their own. They must learn to integrate multiple ideas at the same time and to think abstractly. They have moved out of the stage in which they could process only one idea at a time, and they are graduating from simple, hands-on experiments to hypothetical thinking. They are asking themselves, "What would happen if …?" They can conduct experiments in their head now. They can also learn from watching others' experiences. The intellectual processes in learning expand dramatically in complexity and breadth.

One strange aspect of teenage growth is also occurring. Parts of the teen brain do not function the same way they will in adulthood. The prefrontal cortex—the CEO of the brain that evaluates risk and formulates plans and schedules—is still developing, even up to about age twenty-five. For a time, other parts of the brain are recruited to do some of the work the prefrontal cortex will do in the future.[13] That means you'll see some odd behavior, such as risk-taking and lack of impulse control that will make you wonder about your child's decision-making abilities. But the reason their decisions don't look like yours is that they aren't using their brains the way you do.[14] Knowing this, you can empathize with them, even when you are handing out consequences for poor choices they make.

Another fascinating aspect of intellectual development at this stage is that kids temporarily use a different part of the brain to read other people's emotions.[15] This is why teenagers often cannot accurately perceive other people's facial expressions, body language, or tone of voice. You'll hear them say, "That teacher hates me" or "So-and-so doesn't want to have anything to do with me." This may be because they are not properly interpreting the intentions of the people with whom they are in contact, even those they see daily. Researchers have run experiments in which both adults and teenagers are shown pictures of people expressing fear, anger, and other emotions. Teenagers often mislabel emotions that adults can correctly identify.

Moral growth during the teenage stage begins to expand beyond the strict sense of rules-based "fairness" developed in the elementary stage. Teens will realize that the same hard-and-fast rules can't apply to everyone across the board. They will also see the world isn't necessarily fair. Perhaps they have seen an example in your parenting—that you're more interested in doing what's best for each child than in being "fair." In fact, you should have multiple opportunities in this stage to explain this concept to your kids. They will likely be ready for those discussions because they probably have seen the shortcomings of a rule-based mentality in relationships inside and outside the family.

They will look for principles to live by, and this moral challenge tracks right along with their relational and intellectual development. During the bonding, puppy-love phase of their teenage years, their "love" for the other initially replaces fairness as the highest and best standard for defining right and wrong. As they move into group relationships, good or bad is mostly defined by the group's standards. But as they try out these different possible standards, none will measure up and they will realize that neither hard-and-fast rules nor the opinions of others are sufficient. What they need are general *principles* that can be applied in many different situations. They need a value system that will allow them to discriminate between those things that are godly and those that are worldly.

When the religious leaders asked Jesus which commandment was most important, He gave two answers: love the Lord your God with all your heart, soul, and mind and love others as yourself. (See Matt. 22:36–39.) Like the golden rule—do to others as you would have them do to you—these kinds of broad principles can be applied and expressed in an infinite number of ways. By the end of this stage, your teens will have adopted a value system that depends on a few solid principles. Hopefully, they will learn to apply those principles to each situation hypothetically, analyzing before they act. When they are able to do that more often than not, you will know they have reached the end of the stage. They are ready to move on with their lives, and you will have been their counselor, advisor, and confessor along the way. You can feel confident they have the principles they need for life outside your home. Our prayer is that the principles they adopt are biblically based and that our kids apply them to all of their relationships: family, other individuals, and groups.

## Bringing It Home

Understanding the developmental stages helps us establish reasonable expectations for our children. When we understand the relational, intellectual, and moral struggles they are experiencing at each stage, we can be much more empathetic and supportive. It helps to know that a lot of the quirky, seemingly random things they do are really part of a God-designed process to turn them into the adults He wants them to be.

We also need to remember that our kids go through these stages as amateurs. They aren't going to get it right every time. There is a lot of trial and error. Sometimes, they will seem rude and insensitive when that is not their intention. They are experimenting, and they aren't very good at it yet.

It can be harder to extend empathy to kids in the teenage stage because they look like adults. Our tendency is to attribute adult-like thought processes when they are still growing and maturing. Their thought processes will start to make sense if you understand what they are going through. The bonding they experience with friends in their teenage years may hurt our feelings as parents, but bonding is a skill and they won't often be very balanced until they have had multiple chances to practice that skill. As always, empathy will help them through the teenage awkwardness.

# CHAPTER 10

OBEDIENCE

REBELLION

RESPECT

# CHOICES, CHOICES

WORLDLINESS

Julie felt overwhelmed during her first week of college. She was anxious about all the responsibilities that had suddenly been thrust on her. She had so many decisions to make—deciding on a major, choosing classes, and picking a meal plan. In addition, she was worried about going shopping with her roommate to set up their room. Would her budget cover what she needed?

After looking forward to being on her own, she was beginning to realize how much she had depended on her parents to make decisions for her. They always had strong opinions, and most of the time, it had been easier to go along than to argue. Now Julie was expected to make her own decisions. She wasn't used to weighing pros and cons. What if she made mistakes? Julie could feel her anxiety climbing.

## The Experience of Making Choices

We want our children to grow up to be adults who are capable of solving problems and making good decisions—to be "wise," as the Proverbs say. But as we've seen, this wisdom doesn't happen overnight; it's a process that takes years of practice. If you want your kids to learn to make good choices, it helps to practice how it's done while you're around to guide them. As parents, we can help this process along by giving our kids lots of age-appropriate choices. Instead of taking over their lives and preventing mistakes, we can walk alongside them, setting good boundaries, and allow them to see how the consequences of their choices play out.

Making choices teaches kids how to weigh the options and make decisions in real-life situations. They don't have to be big choices; little ones work too. The point is to give your kids some control over their lives so they can learn how to exercise that control wisely. Our goal is to prepare them for the future when they will have bigger choices to make. Remember when you learned a new skill, such as playing tennis, trying a new recipe, or driving a car? Verbal instruction only took you so far. At some point, you needed hands-on experience to master the skill. Decision making is no different. It requires the opportunity to practice.

Parents who protect their children from making poor choices, either by rescuing or dictating, actually *hinder* their growth because the children don't have the opportunity to take ownership of their choices, priorities, and beliefs. Instead of gaining valuable decision-making experience at home under their parents' roof, these kids will have to go through the learning process as young adults away from home where their mistakes may be major, life-altering decisions. Wouldn't you prefer for your children to struggle with less significant, age-appropriate choices early in their lives and slowly work their way up to bigger decisions while you are there to guide and encourage them?

## Transferring Control

Allowing your kids to make meaningful choices means being willing to relinquish some of your control. When your kids are little, you have a lot of control over their lives. As they grow, however, they become more independent and you will find you have less actual control. They progress from an infant in a crib to a child who becomes more mobile by crawling, walking, and then running. Then they are off to preschool or day care and from there to kindergarten, elementary school, and high school. When they can drive, your level of control drops dramatically. Next thing you know, they're moving out to attend college or start a job.

Almost every day, there is a movement in your kids away from dependence on you. As difficult as it seems at times, your job is to facilitate this movement. This process is easier when parents understand that it is normal and natural for children to exert their independence. They are learning who God made them to be, and at times, they will not view the world as you do. While it's true that kids need adults to guide them along the way, too often that guidance is given with a condescending and controlling spirit. In contrast, giving your children more choices sends the message that you want them to learn to think for themselves.

When you embrace the process of individuation (becoming a separate, unique individual) by giving up appropriate amounts of control, you help *preserve* your relationship with your children. When your kids sense that you see them as unique individuals, they are more likely to talk with you about the decisions they are contemplating. Parents can miss that opportunity if their kids feel micromanaged or disrespected for trying out different views and ideas.

The Bible recognizes that choices are a crucial part of the human experience and each of us is ultimately responsible for the consequences of our choices. This is dramatically demonstrated in Joshua's appeal to the Israelites. Joshua 24:15 reads, "Choose for yourselves this day whom you will serve, whether the God your forefathers served beyond the river, or the gods of the Amorites, in whose land you are living." Chapter 18 of Ezekiel contains God's decree that both fathers and children will be held individually accountable for their choices. Romans 14:12 says, "Each of us will give an account of himself to God." When we give our kids choices and allow them to learn from the consequences, we encourage personal accountability and train them for the days ahead when their choices will have bigger consequences.

## Guidelines for Giving Choices

We're often asked how early the transfer of control should start, and there's no reason why it shouldn't start as soon as kids are old enough to make choices. Giving choices can begin as early as they are able to communicate, so long as the choices are appropriate to the child's age, physically and developmentally. Choices must also fit the level of maturity. That's why it's important to know about the developmental stages—so we can understand which choices are developmentally appropriate.

That does not mean we are hands-off parents, however. We cannot and will not offer our kids *every* possible choice. We are only going to give the choices we are willing for our kids to make within the boundaries we establish. Our authority should be expressed by the setting of boundaries for their choices rather than by making the choices for them. As our children demonstrate an ability to handle responsibility within these boundaries, we can offer them increasing levels of control through more generous boundaries.

Here are some examples of age-appropriate choices for younger kids:

- "Would you like to brush your teeth starting with the bottom or the top teeth first?"
- "Will you start with your carrots or your broccoli?"
- "Rather than watching TV, would you like to play dress up or play with the puzzles?"
- "Would you like to get into the car seat by yourself or would you like some help?"

As they grow, the choices for older kids should become more significant and allow them to exercise more control over their lives. After all, they are getting closer to the time when they will leave home, and the decisions they make should prepare them for that time. For example, letting teenagers choose their extracurricular activities can be an age-appropriate choice. When the schedule allows time for only a couple of activities, let your children decide which one or two they want to do. Instead of trying to convince them to do the activities you prefer, be willing to help them explore their options by asking questions, such as, "How do you think that would work out?" Other examples of choices you can give older kids include deciding whether they want to go out with friends on Friday or Saturday night and whether to work on their term papers on weeknights or on the weekend. Again, this doesn't mean giving them free rein to choose anything they want anytime they want it but rather giving them choices within your boundaries.

One guideline to follow as you give your children more choices is to keep the end goal in mind.

## LEE'S BOX

When you start giving choices, it is important to have a goal in mind and to offer choices that help your child accomplish this goal. I'll share some examples. With a child who doesn't want to go to bed on time, you could say, "Do you want to go to bed with the night light on or off?" The goal is going to bed on time, and the child is given choices that ensure the goal will be achieved while leaving some of the circumstances of the process up to the child. An example for an older child might be, "Do you want to mow the lawn or weed the garden?" The goal is getting some help with the yard work, but the choices give the child some control over the process. Look for opportunities to give choices that move them toward your goals, and you will be rewarded with children who grow and mature more readily.

The choices we give should be truly meaningful and challenging. They will vary depending on the age of the child, but they should allow your child to exert a measure of real control over his or her life. The goal is to teach them to look at their options, think about possible consequences, and learn how to make wise decisions. We can help them down that path by expanding their choices in appropriate increments.

Of course, we will never give choices that jeopardize the child's physical or spiritual safety. The physical safety limit is obvious. We certainly don't want to give our kids choices that could injure them. Good parenting requires physical protection. But we also don't want them to suffer spiritual harm, and that's where a value system comes in. You'll have negotiable and nonnegotiable boundaries that reflect your belief system. You may give a wide range of options in a given situation, but you will not want any of them to be immoral or unethical. You'll want all the options to fit within your values. For example, it may be a family value that everyone goes to church on Sunday. That is not negotiable. But you may be willing to give your kids a choice, and therefore a learning opportunity, by asking them whether they want to go to the 9:30 am service or the one at 11:00 am. You give them a bit of control, but the choices are still within your value system.

As always, our model for perfect parenting is God. He gives us choices and, while His boundaries are often pretty wide, the choices He gives clearly reflect His value system. In the Old Testament, this was crystal clear. Moses went up on Mount Sinai and came back with a "top ten list" displaying God's value system, ranging from God's hatred of idolatry to His basic rules for living. The list became more detailed when God later spelled out more than six hundred additional rules that reflected His standards for right and wrong. But even though there were many rules in the Law, it is still very apparent that God allowed significant space for His people to make choices.

## Expanding and Contracting Boundaries

Releasing control to our children is inevitable for us—and for them. We should learn to do it well rather than postpone or avoid it. This process is a slow, measured release of control—expanding or contracting boundaries based on the choices they make. Hopefully, you will recognize when your kids are ready for a little more responsibility and you will extend it to them. As the central authority, you will evaluate and reevaluate the levels of control they need to move them along the developmental stages. You will weigh how wide your boundaries need to be so your kids will have the opportunity to make significant choices that will teach them valuable life lessons. You will determine the choices that will best teach them about life as believers in a fallen world filled with unbelievers. At the same time, you will have to be sensitive and flexible enough to assess whether the choices you are giving are having the effects you desire.

## MICHELLE'S BOX

Here's an example of restricting the boundaries in response to poor choices: Ten-year-old Gina had a computer in her room and was allowed to play her favorite online game as long as she made doing her homework a priority. Unfortunately, she had trouble shutting down the computer when it was time to do her homework. She said she would turn off the game, but when her mother returned a little while later, she would find Gina still playing. Her mother decided she needed to limit Gina's computer privileges until she could show more responsibility. She said, "I'm so sorry you have chosen to play the game rather than do your homework. I'm going to take away your computer privileges for the next three days. If you can show me that you are responsible enough to respect our limits in other areas during that time, I will give you another chance to balance spending time on the computer and doing your homework."

Here's an example where the parents rewarded good choices by expanding the boundaries: Eight-year-old Robert remembered to do his chores consistently. He went to bed when asked and had no trouble getting up in the morning. Because he handled his responsibilities well, his dad felt Robert was ready to stay up thirty minutes later on weekdays. Instead of focusing his attention just on areas where Robert needed to improve, he was proactive in recognizing and rewarding Robert's strengths. This was really valuable because parents often have the tendency to take positive behavior for granted. When kids make a good effort and it is overlooked, they can become discouraged and lose their motivation.

If your children become overwhelmed by the responsibility of choices, or when they consistently make poor choices, practice a little exploration with them to find out why they are having trouble. Empathetic exploration will give you an opportunity to find out what's going on. It may be that your compliant child is anxious about making decisions and would prefer to be told what to do. While it may feel good to be needed like that, this is not a recipe for long-term success for your child. Reluctant kids must learn to make decisions, and you may have to encourage them to become decision makers. You can let them know you are there to support and offer suggestions by scaffolding if he or she gets stuck.

Rebellious kids rarely need to be pushed into making decisions. Their problem is they tend to overstep your boundaries along the way. Again, empathetic exploration can give you a chance to demonstrate that choices are a privilege that can be abused, and the choices they make will affect the quality of their lives. Exploration will help them evaluate where they might have made a better, more responsible choice. Exploration can also help them understand the factors that motivate poor choices, such as peer pressure, a desire to fit in, control issues, and so forth.

Children who are given lots of choices are more likely to gain a sense of self-control and learn to make better decisions. They become improved problem solvers and better skilled in making responsible decisions during challenging circumstances. Children who aren't allowed to make choices are very likely to seek control in inappropriate ways. When you find yourself constantly battling with your kids over control issues, you may need to look at your parenting style to see if you are contributing to the problem. When your kids are constantly pushing your buttons, you may find it is because they don't feel they have much control over their lives. Some of those families end up in counseling offices because the child's need for control results in some kind of harmful behavior. When these kids feel like the boundaries are too constricted and their thoughts and opinions aren't respected, they may vent their anger and frustration through irresponsible behavior—just to assert their independence.

We know a therapist who saw a family that insisted on counseling because their eight-year-old son wouldn't brush his teeth. The boy excelled at everything else—he was an overachiever at school and was well behaved at home, but he adamantly refused to brush his teeth. After a couple of sessions with the family, the therapist asked the boy why he wouldn't brush. "It's the only thing I can control," the boy said. "They can't *make* me brush my teeth." When kids aren't allowed the freedom to exercise age-appropriate control, they will usually find a way to rebel or retreat.

## Bringing It Home

Choices are so important for a growing child. Without the chance to practice on little choices as a little kid and bigger choices as a bigger kid, it is highly unlikely your kids will become great problem solvers and decision makers magically when they turn eighteen. A lot of trial and error is necessary to learn the skill of decision making. As a parent, you can be a big help if you join your kids as a part of the process, walking with them through the consequences of both good and poor choices.

Some think that giving choices to a child is an abdication of the parents' responsibility and authority, but we think it is just the reverse. If your method of parenting relies only on the kids' immediate obedience to commands, you may find yourself with kids who are unprepared for life without an authority to tell them what to do. Having never had to make choices as a child, they may go looking for a new "authority" to guide them as an adult. Also, having never had to understand why certain choices were better than others, they may be far behind their more experienced peers in developing godly principles to live by and a value system by which to judge their choices.

We believe that a strong authority sets good boundaries for their kids' choices, rather than making the choices for them. That's the job of the central authority—creating an environment within which the child can practice life skills and grow in wisdom. Your relationships with your kids will improve dramatically when you show them that you respect their choices and that you trust God to work in their lives.

# CHAPTER 11

## CONTROL VERSUS INFLUENCE

OBEDIENCE

REBELLION

RESPECT

WORLDLINESS

Jeff was a great kid, but his dad was reaching the end of his rope because Jeff rarely budgeted his time wisely. He always wanted to hang out with his friends or play or practice one of his many sports. Homework didn't seem to be a very big priority and his grades were dropping. Every time his dad emphasized the importance of schoolwork, Jeff said he had it covered. But time and time again, he forgot assignments, and he almost never had time for studying. Exasperated, his dad said, "Why are you being like this? Don't you understand that you won't get into a good college if you keep slacking off? Starting tomorrow, you're coming home right after school and studying till bedtime."

When we get frustrated with our kids, it's a lot easier to issue commands than it is to consider possible choices. Parents often ask us whether there are *any* times when they can just tell their child to do something without having to come up with a choice! For example, what if Mom and Dad have friends on their way to visit and they need the kids to help clean up the house? Giving choices seems like a waste of valuable time because they believe the kids won't do anything. They know the value of choices, but they're in a hurry and wonder, "Is it always necessary to give a choice?"

The answer to this question requires you to look at your overall goal. What are you trying to accomplish as a parent? Certainly there will be times when commands rather than choices are necessary for safety reasons. If your two-year-old is running out in the street, you won't give them a choice! You'll yell, "Stop!" while you try to grab an arm or leg. Your overriding goal is to keep your child safe.

But in a situation like having friends over, you may be tempted to start barking orders when it isn't a matter of life and death. We encourage you to ask yourself whether making demands is really the best way to accomplish your long-term goals for your kids' maturity. Are there some other options besides commands that are more likely to inspire cooperation?

The fact is most commands don't have the effect we hope for anyway. We might think giving a command will solve the problem more quickly, but it often just creates a bigger problem. Commands often lead to control battles that trigger the fight-or-flight response from your kids. Commands can also rob a compliant child of chances to make decisions and learn problem-solving skills because he or she gets used to simply following someone else's orders. And what affect do you think issuing more commands will have on a rebellious child? Most likely, it will only increase his resolve to gain some control in any way he can.

## LEE'S BOX

Sometimes, parents resist giving choices because they feel it undermines their authority. But it's important to remember that when we give commands, we will most likely be met with resistance— either actively or passively. Research shows that when people are given a command, their natural tendency is to want to do the opposite. So when you issue commands, you set the stage for conflict. Giving your kids choices, on the other hand, helps establish a win-win situation. By giving choices, parents help children individuate, practice their decision-making skills, and discover who God designed them to be.

We'll share an example of how giving choices instead of commands can defuse a conflict, maintain the parent's authority, and give the child a chance to run a valuable control experiment. One Sunday after church, Michelle and I went to lunch with Lee and his family. Lee's then four-year-old daughter stood up, sat down, and then tried to walk around the restaurant—the kind of situation in which most parents would demand, "Sit down right now!" But Lee went about it a little differently—and with great effect. He gave his daughter a measure of control, but he did it by offering choices within a range that he was willing to accept. He asked her, "Do you want to sit on your knees or on your bottom?" Michelle and I were amazed when she said, "Bottom," and sat right down. Lee didn't give her a choice between sitting down and running around the restaurant. Running around clearly wasn't a choice he was willing for her to make. But because she had two choices within an acceptable range of options, she felt a sense of control and readily complied—a win/win.

Choices work wonders with older kids too. If you tell a teenager to take out the trash, you may get some resistance. If he reluctantly complies, your request will probably be met with resentment somewhere down the road. Try offering him a choice. "Do you want to take the trash out before dinner or after?" You may be amazed at the results.

## MICHELLE'S BOX

After Chris and I discussed the merits of giving our kids choices, I decided to try it with our seventeen-year-old son. Like most kids that age, he was interested in establishing his independence from me. The result was that my simple requests often turned into control battles. For instance, when I'd tell him to bring in the groceries from the car, he might complain that it was his brother's turn or that he was in the middle of watching television. It was amazing how much more cooperative he was when I rephrased my request in the form of a choice. "Would you rather bring the groceries in now or wait until the commercial?" On one occasion, I asked him if he'd rather wash the car or unload the dishwasher. Either choice was fine with me. I was genuinely surprised when, instead of entering a protracted debate, he simply chose to wash the car.

To become good decision makers, we want our kids to examine the choices they have as they relate to their current circumstances. With this goal in mind, we encourage parents to emphasize choices over obligation. For example, if Darren takes away the remote control from his sister, his mother could yell at him to stop or she could discuss choices with him. "If your sister won't let you watch your program, then taking the remote is an option, but it's probably not a good one because you usually end up fighting. Let's see if we can come up with some better options. What else could you do?" Hopefully, Darren will come up with some alternatives that will work for both him and his sister. If Darren continues to argue and complain rather than trying to resolve the issue, his mother can continue to emphasize choices. "You can choose to keep arguing, but that will mean that you won't be able to use the computer for the rest of the day. You could also choose to figure out how to share the television with your sister which will mean you can keep using the computer."

The key to embracing choices and letting go of controlling attitudes is to realize that the extent of our actual control over our kids is an illusion. Like it or not, you cannot control your child's thoughts, feelings, emotions, and a lot of their actions. When we issue commands, we invite our kids to demonstrate just how little control we truly have. Have you ever said something like "I will not let you talk to me that way"? Many times what you get in response is a child who thinks, *Oh, yeah? You don't want me to yell? Watch this!*

What if we traded our illusion of control for influence? Try shifting your focus from making controlling commands to concentrating instead on what you can control: yourself and your response. Instead of telling your kids what to do, try telling them what *you* will do if they make a good or bad choice. For example, "Don't talk to me that way" is a command that invites the child to demonstrate your inability to control how he speaks to you. But if you say, "I'll be glad to listen as soon as your voice is as soft as mine," you have communicated that you will not continue the discussion until the child can speak to you in a respectful way. You have let go of something you can't control (how they choose to talk) for something you can control (how you will respond). In the process, you have given your child an unspoken choice. "If you want me to talk to you, you will have to choose to speak to me in a respectful way."

Think about the lessons your child is learning from this response. He's learning that communication is a two-way street. Both parties must be respected to have a productive conversation. He's learning that he has control over some things, but he must learn to exercise that control well if he expects a good response from others. He may also learn about delayed gratification because he won't get to vent in the way he wants. He will have to seek some other more mature way to let you know what he feels. And by not engaging in the argument, you are letting your child know that you value a relationship with him and you will not sacrifice any aspect of it by indulging the desire to yell back. Your relationship will be better as you learn to respond to a child's outbursts and bad behavior by telling him how you will respond if he keeps it up. Enjoy watching him react when you try it for the first time. You'll see the wheels turning in his head as he tries to draw you into the control battle he is used to. But stay the course, be empathetic, and remain calm as he tries to retrieve the old parent.

Let's look at some other examples. "Hurry up and finish eating so we won't be late for carpool" is a command, but "The carpool is leaving at 8:00 am, and I hope you've eaten before it leaves" is a choice. Compare "Pick up your dirty clothes" to "I'll be happy to wash the clothes you put in the laundry room." Rather than "Eat your dinner!" what about "I'm happy to serve dessert to everyone who has eaten their dinner"? In all these examples, the parent has emphasized in a calm and nonthreatening voice what he or she will do in response to the kids' behavior. Then follow through with the consequence. Your response will only provide a learning experience if you respect your child's choices enough to deliver the result you promised. If the consequences are not delivered, the choice was not really a choice at all, was it?

## Positive Choices

Another way to influence rather than control your children is through positive choices. We call them positive choices because your response affirms the child's goal and gives choices about how he or she can reach that goal. For example, when the typical parent wants a child to clean up his room before plopping down on the couch, the usual response is worded in a negative way. "You can't lie around on the couch until you clean up your room!" Notice the emphasis is on what the child can't do. What you are saying is, "You cannot sit down and relax right now. What I want you to do is go to your room, make your bed, and

137

straighten everything up right now." The child has two options: obey or rebel. In either case you have encouraged a control battle.

There is a way, however, to maintain your authority and make the same point in a more positive way that discourages control battles. Try a statement like this: "I bet you can't wait to relax a little. As soon as you clean up your room, let's both sit down and rest. Where do you want to start cleaning?" Making a statement like this accomplishes the same purpose—clean up first, then relax—and shows that you recognize and appreciate the child's goals as well. The relationship is improved when your child understands you want the same thing she wants and you will be happy for her when she finishes up her room so she can sit down and relax.

We have a friend who does this very well. She is a single mom with three high-energy boys. When they get off the bus from school, they are ready for some action! They live right next to a park, and their first inclination is to run around that park after a day of sitting in school. When they burst through the door, asking to go out and play, Mom is faced with a lot of pent-up energy. However, for her particular household and kids, she knows it works better for them to do their homework first. Her response is great. She tries to be as energetic as they are and responds by saying, "Absolutely! As soon as you do your homework, you can play outside until dinner." They are much more likely to comply because she has recognized their desire to run and play. Her kids are learning delayed gratification, work ethic, time management, and lots of other lessons, all because Mom has thought about how she wants to respond to her kids—with influence rather than control.

Teaching your kids lessons about adult concepts like time management, a strong work ethic, and delayed gratification may sound far-fetched at first, but these are important disciplines in a culture with a have-it-now mind-set. Did you know that kids who don't learn to delay gratification are the kids most likely to engage in substance abuse? Kids who never learn time-management skills or a strong work ethic are more likely to find college and job responsibilities more difficult than their more disciplined contemporaries. You have an opportunity to help your kids learn these lessons at an early age so they don't have to learn it when the stakes are much higher. We urge you to consider the amount of control you really have, change your mind-set a little, and give these suggestions a try.

## Helpful Guidelines

When you decide to give your kids more choices, it might help to have some practical thoughts to keep in mind. There are a few we have found to be particularly effective. First, when you are giving choices, especially in response to inappropriate requests or behavior, try to remain calm. A calm, empathetic parent is more effective and earns more respect than a parent who loses his or her cool. Staying calm also keeps the focus on the child's choices rather than on your angry reactions.

## Describe the Problem

One way to break out of the command-giving mode is to describe the problem. This helps parents avoid words that blame and focuses instead on what needs to be done. By describing the problem instead of giving a command, you make it easier to think of choices to offer and invite the child to take responsibility. For instance, if a child spills his milk, you could say, "I see the milk spilled. Would you rather wipe it up with a paper towel or use the sponge?" You could say to a teenager who has a messy room, "I see lots of clothes on the floor. Would you rather wash them or hang them up?"

## Have a Time Limit

Give them a time limit to make a choice. In most cases, your kids won't need much time to make the choices you give them. A minute or two usually is all they need, but give them a reasonable time to think through their choices. It may strain your patience, but silence can be your ally as they weigh choices. Don't fill that empty space with suggestions or hints. Let your child choose. If your kids don't choose within a reasonable period, you can say something like "I'm going to have to choose for you this time, but hopefully next time you'll make the choice." That's usually enough to reinforce the importance of their own decision making, especially with a child who is rebelling by intentionally *not* making a choice (a passive-aggressive sort of rebellion).

On the other hand, it is important for your kids to learn that you expect them to make the choices you give them. Some kids become so dependent on their parents they find it difficult to make any choice at all. These kids will ask you to tell them what to do because they have found it easier to cope with life by allowing you to make their choices for them. He or she may say, "I can't decide. Will you help me?" While it can feel pretty good to be the parent who comes up with a solution to every problem, this kind of dependence is not healthy for your child. Think about what could happen when a dependent girl, whose parents have always told her what to do, goes away to college or moves out of town. She's not going to pick up decision-making skills the minute she leaves home. She may look for someone who can take your place and make decisions for her because that's her coping mechanism. Unfortunately, there are plenty of less than honorable people who will volunteer for that job.

If your child has trouble making decisions, ask open-ended questions. "This seems really hard for you. Why do you think you are having a tough time choosing?" Again, use silence as your ally and allow her to explore the root of her indecision. Listen to what she says and help her work through it. Walking through the problem-solving process is a much better response than just giving up and making the decision for her.

## Repeat the Choices

Another practical way to help your kids choose well, especially when they want to add more choices or argue about the ones you gave them, is to ask them to repeat the choices. The act of repeating the choices actually makes it more likely they will choose one. Sometimes, it helps simply to ask, "Can you repeat the choices for me?" and let your kids spell them out. It makes them focus on the more important issue of making a good choice within your boundaries rather than arguing about why they should have other options.

Also, we've found it helpful to give only a couple of choices. That's especially true for young kids. Remember kids under the age of about twelve are concrete thinkers and tend to focus on just one thought or concept at a time. You'll lose them if you give them too many options or expect them to draw their own conclusions. So limit them to two options. For example, you may ask, "Would you like to wear the red dress or the blue one?" Some of us have been blessed with little "lawyers" who, when given the choice between A and B, will ask about C or D or E. The best response to that is, "Yes, I know you like those too, but the choices were A and B. Which one will you choose?"

As kids get older and are able to think abstractly, you can give them more room to come up with their own solutions and negotiate choices. For example, instead of setting a standing curfew, you could talk with your child about their plans for the night and negotiate a reasonable curfew based on the activity. If he violates the agreed-on curfew, you have the chance to talk about making good choices and about the consequences of poor ones. "I see that you chose to stay out longer than the curfew we agreed on, so let's talk about consequences and how you might be able to reestablish trust for the future. In the meantime, I'm going to set the curfews for you."

## First-Time Obedience

Occasionally, we are asked about the concept of "first-time obedience" and whether we are in favor of it or not. "First-time obedience" insists that a child does whatever the parent tells him to do without challenge, excuse, or delay. While it sounds like a good idea—after all, who doesn't want first-time obedience?—let's look at what this concept really implies. It is essentially a command because no choice is given, the child must obey, and obedience must come quickly—without question, argument, negotiating, or delay. But is it the best way for them to learn crucial decision-making skills? Obviously not. When you provide choices, you engage developing brains and provide opportunities to learn how to solve problems and make decisions.

Another problem with "first-time obedience" is the relational effect. Although parents must be the central authorities in the home, does demanding obedience really earn respect and draw kids into authentic relationship? If you want to be a counselor to your kids and engage in real discussions about important issues that affect their lives, it would seem that giving a child choices will provide greater opportunities to have these conversations. By doing so, you are not holding yourself out as the only source of control in the relationship. Instead, you are acknowledging that your children need to have some control over their lives to grow and mature, and that you are okay with that. They will feel respected when they see that you have confidence in their ability to make the choices you give them. With commands and first-time obedience, instead of laying the foundation for an authentic relationship, you're likely to end up in a control battle.

Because commands require immediate obedience, they are essentially a bid to take control of the situation. Is it too radical to suggest that we stop thinking about how to control our kids and start thinking about how we can influence them toward the kind of behavior that pleases God? If you think about it, only God has complete control, yet He almost never uses it to make us do His will. If God isn't using the concept of first-time obedience, why should we?

## Bringing It Home

Choices are a great way to give your kids a measured and appropriate amount of control so they can learn to become better problem solvers and decision makers. For dictators who are used to controlling everything, giving more choices can be difficult. They will get frustrated watching their kids struggle and will think they can do it better and faster than their kids. But taking over the problem isn't the point of good parenting.

Rescuers who don't like to see their kids experience the negative consequences of their choices will want to protect them and prevent pain. Their challenge is to understand how choices play a huge part in the process God has set in place to mature their kids into adults.

Many parents feel that giving more choices to their kids is an abdication of their parental duties. For these parents, it seems they have given up their God-given position and authority. That taps into the old mind-set that says, "I am in control here, and I have the duty to make my kids do what is best for them." But the truth is we really cannot control everything our kids do and control battles erupt almost every time we try. If we change our mind-set about parental authority so that we gradually release an appropriate amount of control to our kids, we are much closer to God's example. Giving our kids more control of their lives in measured, age-appropriate ways can teach them the problem-solving skills they will need for the rest of their lives. It will help us show them in a significant way that we are on their side, and it will go a long way toward defusing control battles.

# CHAPTER 12

## SOWERS MUST REAP

Ann had just turned fifteen and desperately wanted a new, top-of-the-line smart phone. Many of her friends had one and she was sure she couldn't live one more day without it. Her parents were reluctant, having heard a lot of stories about kids using the text and e-mail features, Internet, video camera, and downloadable applications to do inappropriate things. Still, she was well behaved and hardly ever got into trouble, so they relented with the provision that, because they were paying for the phone, Ann would share all messages she sent and received.

A couple of weeks later, Ann's mom saw a text message as it flashed on the screen of the new phone. The text came from a boy at school and the contents shocked her. She called for Ann to come into the kitchen and asked her to open up her text messages. Complaining about the invasion of privacy, Ann reluctantly opened her messages. Her mom started reading the strings of exchanges on the phone. The boy was sexting (sending graphic, sexually charged messages), and Ann had responded likewise. Ann's mom was horrified. What should she do? She was angry but also knew she needed to do some empathetic exploration to find out why Ann responded to these texts. She knew she would need to come up with some consequences. She decided to give herself time to calm down and wait for her husband to come home so they could have a team meeting to decide the best course of action.

## Teaching Lessons through Consequences

Giving choices to our kids is an important part of their maturing process, but choices aren't made in a vacuum. To be effective, they must be accompanied by another element that's vital to our children's maturity: consequences. Every decision in life has consequences—good or bad. In most cases, the choices we make have a direct effect on the quality of our lives because of the resulting consequences. Our kids need to be very familiar with this dynamic because it is one of the basic principles of life that people usually reap what they sow. We can help them learn this lesson by letting them experience the real life consequences of their choices in a way that illustrates the reaping and sowing principles and prepares them for life on their own.

As we mentioned before, kids are expected to seek greater amounts of independence to discover who they are apart from their parents. This is a normal and natural process. They will make some mistakes along the way. That's expected. Our goal as parents is to use those mistakes as opportunities to teach important lessons in a loving and empathetic way. Most of us can remember a time when we violated boundaries or made irresponsible decisions as we were growing up. And if we're honest, we *still* test the limits with our heavenly Father. Just as God disciplines us when we violate His boundaries by sinning, we have the responsibility to deliver appropriate consequences to our kids when they violate our boundaries. That's how they discover whether their choices are good or bad.

## Follow Through

Many parents struggle with giving consequences to their kids. Why? Some parents are afraid their kids will get angry. Others are afraid consequences will disappoint or discourage their kids. Still others worry that consequences may cause their kids to miss out on something other kids are enjoying. In each of these cases the focus is on the present dilemma. But if our goals are eternally focused, we have to stop looking at each situation as if the happiness of our kids or our own comfort is the most important factors. Reminding yourself that you are parenting for eternity can help you focus your attention on *what* your kids can get out of a trial rather than *how* they can get out of it. It's often better in the long run for our kids to experience the consequences of their choices than for them to be comfortable and content in the moment. This takes a lot of strength, however.

So the first step in following through with consequences is to consider them as teaching opportunities, not as punishment. The goal is to use the consequences of a bad choice to teach a lesson that will benefit your child in the long run. Think about it as God does.

> It is for discipline that you have to endure. God is treating you as sons. For what son is there whom his father does not discipline? ... Besides this, we have had earthly fathers who disciplined us and we respected them. Shall we not much more be subject to the Father of spirits and live? For they disciplined us for a short time as it seemed best to them, but he disciplines us for our good, that we may share his holiness. For the moment all discipline seems painful rather than pleasant, but later it yields the peaceful fruit of righteousness to those who have been trained by it.
>
> Hebrews 12:7, 9–11

Also consider Romans 8:28. "We know that in all things God works for the good of those who love him, who have been called according to his purpose." Your children's poor choices and the resulting consequences can work "good" for them.

## Consistency Is Key

As part of a behavioral study, researchers conducted an experiment on pigeons.[16] In the first stage, when the pigeons pecked a target, a food pellet would come out. The birds quickly learned that a particular behavior (pecking the target) resulted in a certain consequence (food pellets). In the second stage, the researchers removed the pellets. After numerous attempts at pecking the target in vain, the pigeons figured out that pecking no longer resulted in a food pellet, so they stopped pecking altogether. In the final stage, the researchers delivered food pellets based on pecking the target, but not consistently. Sometimes, pecking would result in a pellet; other times, not. The reward was made random and arbitrary to see how the pigeons would react. What was the result? The researchers discovered that the pigeons pecked even more—up to four thousand times per hour! Just the *possibility* that a food pellet might come out was enough for them to persist through many futile attempts. Inconsistency made the pigeons try *harder*, hoping for the exception to the rule.

The study reaffirms the value of consistency in consequences. Consistent consequences change behavior. While it is important to explore the children's motivation for their behavior, it is also important for them to know what will happen when they make those choices. If consequences are not consistent, how can we expect children to understand why they shouldn't make the same choice again? We confuse the child when a certain behavior elicits a spanking one day, a lecture the next, a stern warning the third, and nothing on the fourth. Teaching is obscured by unpredictable consequences.

When we are consistent in delivering consequences without rescuing or dictating, our kids will learn the lesson we most want to teach—that their choices significantly affect the quality of their lives. However, if we rescue, dictate, or forego consequences some of the time, we can expect our kids to spend far more time "pecking the target" and hoping for relief from consequences than accepting that they made a poor choice and now have to face a consequence.

The story of Moses' disobedience in the wilderness (Num. 20:1–13) is a great example of God's consistency in delivering consequences to His children, regardless of their rank, standing, or prior obedience. You'll recall that Moses was faithful to God for many years. He had led God's people out of Egypt, through the parting of the Red Sea, almost into the Promised Land, and then back into the wilderness for many years after the people were disobedient again. But at one point in their journey, when the fickle Israelites complained about a lack of water in the desert of Zin, Moses lost his cool. God had given him instructions on how He would provide water from a rock, but Moses, venting his anger at the people and the situation, struck the rock with his staff and took credit for providing the water rather than giving the glory and honor to God. As a result, God delivered a consequence to Moses. Neither he nor his brother Aaron would be allowed to enter the Promised Land. That was God's consequence for Moses' lack of humility and inability to control his anger!

That's a powerful example. If I had been God in that situation, I would have had a hard time giving Moses much of a consequence. After all, he had endured a lot from the Israelites' constant complaining and rebellion—enough to make anyone angry. God had entrusted him with the leadership and destiny of His people. For the most part, Moses had been a righteous man who followed God's direction despite challenging and dangerous circumstances. When God first called to him at the burning bush, Moses complied with God's directions despite his uncertainty and fear. Now, however, he had lost his temper and God held him accountable. He was prevented from entering the Promised Land—the single goal of his life for more than forty years. But God was focused on the eternal perspective rather than on making Moses happy for his short time on earth. After all, Moses eventually entered the Promised Land when he went to heaven. The consequences delivered to Moses were a lesson for him, his followers, and for all of us who read the account.

The most significant lesson we can learn from this story is that God parents us to prepare us for eternity with Him. Clearly, He is less concerned with our temporary status in this world than he is with our status as citizens of His supernatural world. His perspective places no value on money, power, beauty, or fame because those things do not translate to eternity. Faith, hope, and love are the values God wants for us, and Moses failed to display those attributes in his disobedient action. Instead of humbly trusting God's instructions for dealing with the situation, he took credit for the miraculous act.

Shouldn't we take our cues from God and have the same perspective for our children? Are we more concerned for their momentary happiness or for building character and helping them learn to make choices that have an eternal impact? When we are unwilling to address poor choices with consequences in relatively minor events or issues, we may be setting them up to make major mistakes that will have lasting results.

## Letting It Slide

Sometimes, we are asked if it is okay to forego consequences every now and then. Usually, this question is presented one of two ways: either the child is so good most of the time that it seems unloving to deliver consequences on those rare occasions when she actually makes a poor choice or the parent believes he can teach the child the concept of grace by *not* delivering a consequence. The problem, in either case, is that the parent introduces inconsistency into the consequences equation. Being parents ourselves, we know how hard it is to be consistent with consequences, especially big ones, but we also know from experience that inconsistency usually ends up being more painful for both us and our children. Inconsistency means it will take additional painful instances of giving and receiving consequences for the same lesson to be learned.

So let's look at the two examples above. First, with a compliant, well-behaved child, you will find you have fewer opportunities to teach lessons based on poor choices. They don't make many! But isn't that a reason to be more consistent with consequences rather than less? After all, you won't have as many opportunities to teach your compliant children as those of us with rebellious kids. And compliant kids are more likely to take the lessons to heart because they want to please you. You are really doing them a tremendous favor when you deliver consequences on those rare occasions when they mess up. It is the most loving thing you can do for them.

In the second example, where the parent tries to teach the concept of grace by foregoing consequences, we have a different issue altogether. We assume the parent would explain to the child that he made a poor choice and a consequence is due, but the parent has decided to forego the consequences just as God did when He sent His Son as a substitute to die for the sins of the world. The question is whether the lesson is a legitimate one and whether the doctrine of God's grace is really being conveyed. Here's the problem: God's saving grace is of a different nature altogether from a parent's action in foregoing consequences. God's saving grace restores our relationship with Him and keeps us from being separated from the family of God for eternity. It does not save us from the consequences of our sin. Even believers reap what they sow. The Bible is full of God delivering consequences for sin, even the sin of believers. Ananias and Sapphira can testify to that. (See Acts 5:1–11.) Confusing consequences with saving grace can result in kids who expect God to save them from reaping what they sow—an expectation that will certainly disappoint them throughout their lives.

The better course of action is to deliver the consequences rather than avoiding the issue. Practically speaking, it prepares your kids for life in the real world. When we forego consequences at home, we condition our kids to expect the same from other authorities in their lives. Giving consequences in the supportive, loving atmosphere of your home teaches lessons that will likely reduce the number of times they will have to receive consequences from others.

Consistent consequences actually communicate love to your kids. They show you care enough about them to address their behavior. As always, empathy is the essential element in delivering consequences. Your empathy will make them better able to focus on the issue at hand because you have communicated your love for them—that you believe they can learn from the experience and that you are on their team while they struggle. Show your children that you feel sadness for their poor choices and that you are greatly encouraged by their good ones, and they will feel your unconditional love and support in spite of the choices they have made. That's a model of God's parenting style!

## LEE'S BOX

I have a friend who was adopted. She remembers the moment when she first felt like an integral part of her adopted family. Her mother had told her no to something she wanted, and she responded with the meanest comment she could think of: "I hate you, and you're *not* my mother!" The mother's response demonstrated she knew the most loving thing she could do for her daughter was to hold firm on her boundary, even if it was painful at the time. With tears in her eyes, her mother answered, "Sweetheart, I love you so much I'm willing to let you hate me in order to do what's best for you." My friend says she never felt more secure than she did at that moment.

## Which Consequences Are Best?

If consequences are a crucial element of experience, you've probably guessed that designing and delivering good consequences is very important. In some cases, the consequences will occur naturally, such as when a teacher disciplines your child for disobedience at school. But other times, you will be required to come up with a consequence that fits the "crime" and deliver it in a way that reinforces the lesson. Maximizing the teaching opportunities will require some thought rather than just defaulting to the same consequence time after time. Michelle and I tried using grounding (confining our kids to the house for periods of time) as our default consequence. We grounded our kids for every transgression. But eventually, we realized this wasn't always the most effective way to teach the lessons we wanted our sons to learn. Instead, we began to consider ways to use different consequences to demonstrate how the outside world would respond to them in a similar situation. Chores and service projects are a couple of examples.

## Natural Consequences

Sometimes, consequences are imposed by authorities, such as teachers, coaches, or administrators. When your child misbehaves at school and earns detention, you don't have to do anything further to make the point. The consequences are "natural" because all you have to do is let them unfold. In these cases, the best thing you can do is to allow your child to talk about the situation and reflect their feelings back to him. "You are really angry you got detention for being five minutes late." Avoid the temptation to blame the authority. More importantly, avoid the temptation to reinforce the lesson by making judgmental comments such as "I've told you time and time again that you need to leave the house earlier." While these kinds of statements may lower our anxiety as parents, they shut down authentic communication. Let the natural consequences do the teaching instead. After your child has vented, you can gently lead him through an exploration of the motivations behind the behavior that got him in trouble. This might sound something like "You really hate going to detention. What do you think you're going to do differently to avoid it in the future?"

Rather than just telling your children they need to get up earlier and make a better effort to be on time, let *them* do the problem solving. We encourage this process by asking open-ended questions. This leads them to look at the choices that resulted in a consequence. In our heightened anxiety over our children's misbehavior, we often hastily connect the dots for them. But instead of leading them to a better understanding of their poor choices, this usually causes them to defend their behavior even more vigorously.

I learned a great lesson from natural consequences when I turned sixteen. I desperately wanted my own car. Though a lot of my friends had "muscle" cars—common in the rural Ohio farmland where I lived—I really wanted a sports car. Specifically, I wanted a Triumph Spitfire. As far as I knew, there wasn't a Spitfire within fifty counties. But I had my mind set on getting one and eventually I found a five-year-old model for $850. The fact that Spitfires were notorious for breaking down didn't deter me. I wanted that car!

In their great wisdom, my parents didn't prevent me from buying the car. I'm pretty sure they knew I was making a bad decision. But they understood that my experience would be a far better teacher than a lecture on how to look for and buy a car. They agreed to cosign a loan as long as I had a job to pay it back. That was about as far as their involvement went. They basically said, "Good luck. Hope it works out for you." You can guess what happened. While my new sports car looked like a Triumph Spitfire on the outside, it was basically junk on the inside! It ran for only a couple of weeks at a time before it needed extensive repairs, none of which I was capable of doing by myself. The car had a cool radio too—very important for a teenager—but whoever installed it must have done a pretty quick wiring job, because, one time in the dead of winter, my radio caught fire. The wiring sparked, smoke started billowing, and my car looked like a smoke bomb rolling down the road.

As I said, I suspect my parents knew what I was getting into. They could have tried to prevent me from making a mistake, but they recognized that natural consequences would be my best teacher. They were right. While my experience was painful at the time, it helped me better understand how to make good buying decisions in the long run. Because they let me experience the natural consequences, I learned how to buy a car (or how *not* to buy one). I also learned an important lesson about the difference between instant gratification and a more reasoned approach to things I wanted. My parents didn't have to say a word about it. They let me have the experience and empathized with the predictable consequences of my choices.

## Logical and Reasonable Consequences

Natural consequences are great, and they make our job as parents easier, but they don't always occur. When natural consequences aren't forthcoming, you will have to impose the consequences yourself. When these situations arise, there are two criteria for coming up with effective consequences: they should be logical and reasonable. Logical consequences are most like what would happen in the real world as a result of similar behavior. For instance, when a child throws a tantrum, she might be sent to her room. That consequence is logical because a person who acts out in real life is likely to be isolated by his or her peer group. A teenager caught drinking and driving might find himself without driving privileges and stuck at home, imitating the natural consequences of a DUI.

## MICHELLE'S BOX

When Chris and I got creative, we were better able to come up with consequences that related to the offense. For example, when our boys were teenagers, we found ourselves constantly cleaning up empty cups and wrappers and bits of sandwiches from around the computer in our home. I would feel resentful every morning having to clean up the mess the boys had left the night before. So one day, I decided to give some choices. I woke up my oldest son, Ben, one morning and asked if he would rather clean up the computer area or pay me fifteen dollars to do it. I was okay with the fifteen-dollar fee because I figured that would let me relax and buy a nice lunch and a cup of coffee.

"I'm not paying fifteen dollars," he answered.

"Great. You'll clean it up then?" I asked.

"No, I don't want to do that either. Come on, I'm tired and I just want to go back to sleep."

I made it clear he would have to do one or the other and assured him that either way was fine with me, so he finally agreed to pay, probably just to get back to sleep. I cleaned up the mess in about five minutes. When he woke up later that morning, I reminded him that he owed me fifteen dollars.

He began to object. "I was still in my REM cycle! I didn't know what I was agreeing to. Fifteen dollars is ridiculous!"

At that point, everything in me wanted to launch into a lecture about how I had been cleaning up the mess for the last couple of months, how I had given him a clear choice, and how he didn't appreciate all the work I did around the house. Somehow, I resisted the urge and remained calm. Still, he insisted he wouldn't pay.

That's a definite boundary violation. To be honest, I had no idea what to do, but I managed to stay calm. I walked downstairs and made lunch. This confused Ben because this was *not* the way I normally handled conflict. While I sat down to eat my lunch, he stared at me with a perplexed look on his face and said, "Why are you sitting there all calm-like!" I said, "I just know your choice not to pay isn't going to be good for you."

When Chris came home, we discussed the issue. Ben made a poor choice that needed to be addressed. We wanted to use this experience to teach good life lessons. After discussing the issue in private, we came up with a plan. Our son is an artist and he had quite a few paintings lying around the house. We decided to "foreclose" on one of his paintings to show him the consequences of reneging on a promise to pay. Chris took one of his better paintings to his office. We wrote out a foreclosure notice that said we would return the painting to him once he paid the fifteen dollars he owed *plus* a five-dollar processing fee for the hassle of having to resort to foreclosure. If he didn't pay by the end of the next week, we would sell the painting at an auction, deduct the amount he owed, and give him any proceeds over and above twenty dollars. We were in the middle of an eight-week parenting seminar, so if it came to that, we had a ready audience for the auction. We handed him the notice and let him read it. Of course, he thought it was outrageous. But we were firm; he owed the money and refused to pay so foreclosure was our only option. And he was just as firm that he wouldn't pay.

He thought our action was unfair. We told him how sorry we were that he was in this predicament and reassured him that he could solve the problem by paying the debt. The standoff continued until about 6:45 pm on the very last day when he reluctantly paid the debt. That was the end of it too. No more arguments. No grumbling. It was over because we were empathetic but firm.

To be truthful, the foreclosure process was kind of fun for us because it gave us a chance to teach a variety of lessons that went beyond the immediate issue. He had clearly crossed a line by refusing to pay for the cleanup and we dealt with that. But he also got to learn what happens when you don't pay what you owe. In the real world when you renege on a debt, people foreclose. They usually don't care why you can't pay; they just want their money. These are painful lessons, but our son learned them in a fairly harmless way under our roof.

"Reasonable" consequences are those that are appropriately strict for the offense. The punishment should fit the crime, so to speak. When Michelle and I used grounding as our default consequence, our lack of imagination meant we were forced sometimes to stack consequences on top of consequences if a new violation occurred before the last sentence was up. If you do that often enough, your kids will begin to wonder if they are stuck in a third-world prison system. After a month or two, a bad choice that causes an extra week's grounding isn't a learning experience. Their poor choice can be forgotten in the interminable discipline. What should have been a learning opportunity turns into an extended season of being stuck in one big consequence.

In addition to an overly lengthy consequence, there are times when you may overreact in the heat of the moment and deliver a consequence that's too harsh. Some kids have a knack for using a parent's propensity to anger as a way to avoid having to deal with the consequences of poor choices. They know how to push the buttons that will cause Mom or Dad to explode, start yelling, and hand out onerous consequences. The kids also know that when the situation blows over, Mom or Dad will realize the consequences are too harsh and relent or perhaps even forget them altogether. The bonus is that during the parental explosion, they don't have to face the fact they made a bad choice. They can focus all the attention on the overreacting parent.

The learning experience is also diminished when a consequence is too lenient. A consequence that's too harsh turns the focus on you—you become the "mean" mom or Dad—but a consequence that's too weak will cause the focus to be lost altogether. Your kids may be willing to make the same bad choices again because they can easily endure the results. An introverted kid may actually *enjoy* the solitude and quiet of being grounded, for example. Grounding this type of child would not be an effective consequence. When you think about and deliver consequences that are reasonable and naturally tied to the offense, you will see how much more effective they are. For more examples of logical and reasonable consequences, see the appendix at the end of the book.

## Have a Plan Ready in Advance

When emotions are high, it can be difficult to sort through the possible consequences and choose one that fits the situation appropriately.

You may find yourself reacting angrily to your children's moods and behavior rather than calmly leading by example. One way to come up with effective consequences and break out of ingrained unhealthy responses is to plan ahead.

You know your kids. Chances are they have predictable behaviors and patterns that you encounter with regularity. As we mentioned in chapter 8, it's important to consider if your child is getting in trouble because he or she lacks a certain skill. If so, it is a good idea to spend some time helping them learn this skill. But the learning process may also require you to teach by giving consequences. Because you know how your child might behave under a particular set of circumstances, it is very helpful to work together with your spouse or friends and come up with a set of consequences ahead of time before the crisis erupts. When you have a game plan, you will find it much easier to stay calm and deliver the consequences empathetically.

We know a mother whose young child had a difficult time leaving the park when it was time to go. He would cry, throw toys, yell at the other kids, and fall on the ground rather than get in the car. The conflict became a regular routine. So Mom decided to plan ahead. The next time they tried to leave the park and her son started into his customary tantrum, she calmly said, "Oh, I'm so sorry you're choosing to leave this way. We won't be able to come back tomorrow. I hope you can be more calm so we can come back again later this week." The confused son stopped and looked at her. This wasn't the normal scenario where he begged and pleaded, his mother nagged and threatened him, and they eventually ended up staying at the park. Instead, Mom had acknowledged his feelings, but she wasn't budging on the consequence. So the son got in the car. Mom followed through on her word; they didn't go to the park the next day or the next. On the third day, on the way to the park, Mom briefly mentioned how she hoped they wouldn't have a scene when it was time to leave because that would mean they would have to take an even longer break from the park. The son recognized he had a choice to make, and that the quality of his next few days was up to him. Mom didn't try to make him behave, but she let him know what she would do if he didn't. It was easier for her to stay calm because she had a game plan and consequences ready in case she needed them.

## The Right Currency

Consequences are more effective when you know the "currency" of each of your children—the things that are important to them. Every child is different. Some children are focused on money while free time is a more precious commodity for some. For instance, a fifteen-dollar fine will have quite an effect on a child who is money oriented but hardly any on a child who isn't. Likewise, being grounded may have less effect on a child who enjoys staying at home than it does for a child whose social calendar is always booked.

We have included a worksheet in the appendix at the end of the book with recommendations for designing consequences for each of your kids. It is intended to be a conversation starter for you, your spouse, and your friends. It will prompt you to think about each child's particular personality and to talk through the kinds of consequences that are most likely to get that child's attention. It divides possible consequences into four different groups.

- **The things your child doesn't like to do**—chores or time alone in his/her room, for example. For some kids, doing something for others is a very effective consequence because it reminds them that there is a downside to a self-centered attitude. For other kids, time alone focuses their attention on the issue at hand and encourages self-exploration.
- **Things your child likes to do that can be restricted**—cell phones or computer time, for example. These are effective consequences when the poor choices that prompt the consequence are related to overuse of the thing you take away. When texting interferes with homework or bedtime, or online games take the place of chores, a good consequence is to remove the distracting device or activity until your child can show that he or she can be more responsible. It's a great way to demonstrate how the use of cell phones and computers must fit in the overall context of life.
- **The third column includes extra favors or privileges that can be taken away.** Please understand we don't mean that you should spend less time with your kids or punish them by withholding your love—that's much too severe. They should

always be sure they are a part of the family and that you will always love them. But it's appropriate to put on this list some extra activities you might do for them—special trips or stopping for ice cream on the way home from school, for example. These can be withheld when your kids are disrespectful or aren't very pleasant to be around. In the real world, people don't do favors for someone who is whining, complaining, or disrespectful. Taking away one of these favors demonstrates that effectively.

- **The fourth column is for exchanges—chores, favors, and tasks your child can do for you to "compensate" you for doing something they didn't do.** When your child doesn't make his bed and you do it for him, for example, you've spent extra time and energy making up for his bad choice. You can create some opportunities for him to give you back your time and energy by doing one of *your* chores: making dinner, washing the car, etc. This category is generally easier with older kids than younger ones, for obvious reasons. You don't want a two-year-old doing some of your chores. But even with little kids, you can usually find a way to work out an appropriate exchange.

## Bringing It Home

Giving kids more learning opportunities through choices is only effective if we also let them experience the consequences of those choices. Consequences complete the learning experience by showing kids what happens as a result of the choices they make. If we take consequences out of experiential learning, we gut the experience. While we may think we are being more loving by foregoing consequences, we are only ensuring that they will be experienced later in a less supportive atmosphere.

Imaginative consequences that consider how similar choices will play out in the world outside the home are far better than lectures and nagging. Take the time to think about the consequences you deliver to make sure they communicate the lesson you want to teach. While a poor decision should be acknowledged right away, the consequence doesn't have to be delivered in the heat of the moment. You may sometimes want to wait to consult with your spouse or friends and then design your consequence to make the most of the learning opportunity.

Giving consequences with empathy is much easier when we plan ahead. Completing the consequence worksheets will prepare you to handle each child's poor choices effectively. It will also give you more confidence when you face disobedience or disrespect because you will have the consequences handy when you need them. Completing the worksheets should also stir your imagination to come up with creative solutions to the issues your family faces, especially chronic issues.

Consequences are worth the effort. Although we can come up with lots of reasons for avoiding them, consequences are biblical and discipline really is an act of love. God uses our poor choices to teach us. We can do the same for our children. Let's resolve to love our children by using thoughtful consequences delivered empathetically and consistently.

# CHAPTER 13

# DELIVERING CONSEQUENCES

Jim and Nancy had an eight-year-old son with an anger problem. Whenever he got in trouble, he would respond by yelling, crying, stomping his feet, or picking on his little sister. Unfortunately, Jim also had trouble controlling his anger. When his son acted out, Jim would lose his temper. Trying to demonstrate that he was in charge, Jim met his son's anger by upping the ante. Soon they would be shouting at each other with Jim vowing even more consequences if his son kept it up. Most of these arguments ended with Nancy trying to calm Jim down and with their son yelling that his parents were the meanest people he knew. Instead of thinking about the choices he made or the consequences he faced, the son could only think about growing up so his dad couldn't overpower him anymore.

## Exercising Authority Respectfully

Coming up with imaginative, insight-provoking consequences isn't the only challenge. We also need to deliver them well. It's possible to have a great consequence but ruin the teaching opportunity by delivering it in a shaming or belittling way. We battle against selfish human nature when we're interacting with our kids just as we do in our marriages, friendships, or professional relationships. But our position of authority and power over our children makes them particularly vulnerable to how we express our thoughts and opinions. There will be times when you'll be tempted to rant, rave, be sarcastic, or vent your feelings when your kids misbehave. We all are prone to this. But parents can do a great deal of emotional damage when they exert their authority in aggressive and belittling ways. Rather than humbly admitting we are wrong, we will often try to rationalize our misuse of power and force our kids to deal with the negative effects of our actions. Parents need to be safe people whom their kids can trust to provide emotional stability in times of conflict. That is why an important step toward delivering consequences in a healthy way is to look at how you tend to express your anger.

## Healthy and Unhealthy Anger

We've talked about how poor expressions of anger can cause our children to focus on our response instead of their poor choice. But not all anger is bad. Anger is an emotion that motivates us to address problems. Trying to be anger free as a parent is not a realistic goal. The Bible recognizes the reality of anger when it says, "Be angry and yet do not sin." (Eph. 4:26). James 1:19 states, "Let everyone be quick to hear, slow to speak, and slow to anger." Ephesians 4:15 mentions "speaking the truth in love." The emphasis isn't on the elimination of anger but on expressing it in a godly way. Unfortunately, when we don't muster the strength to follow through with needed consequences, we can become resentful and this pent-up anger can manifest itself in unhealthy ways.

Here are three ways that anger is mismanaged (excerpted from the book *The Anger Workbook for Christian Parents*, by Les Carter and Frank Minirth). The first is **suppressing anger**. In a desire to avoid the painful and destructive sides of anger, some parents refuse to admit they are angry and resolve to keep it buried inside. Here are some of the characteristics of a parent who suppresses anger:

- avoids conversations that *could* lead to conflict
- is image conscious and wants to appear in control
- is reluctant to be direct about hurts or needs
- deliberately avoids conflict

- hides feelings of confusion or hurt
- lets hours or days go by without telling anyone about a hurt
- holds onto resentments
- appeases others to make conflict go away
- feels paralyzed when confronted with unwanted situations

Suppressed anger is quietly harbored, but it does not dissolve. The very pain that is momentarily avoided is usually experienced by the angry person at a later date. People who handle their anger this way are more susceptible to depression and disillusionment.

Another way anger is mismanaged is through **openly aggressive anger**. It may be prompted by a legitimate cause, but aggressive anger shows little or no regard for the needs of the other people involved. Some characteristics of openly aggressive anger are

- blunt and abrasive speech
- physically abusive behavior, like shoving or throwing things
- insulting words or foul language
- loaded questions meant to demean another ("What's wrong with you?")
- accusation or blame
- being critical as opinions are expressed
- open defiance and lack of cooperation
- condescension

Openly aggressive people often assume the only way to have their needs addressed is by overpowering others. Behind their forcefulness is a fear that a calmer approach will not bring about the results they desire. In the short run, forceful anger may gain compliance, but over the course of time, relationships are sure to be damaged.

**Passive-aggressive anger** is a third way anger is mismanaged. The aggressive element is less overt; instead, the passive-aggressive person expresses anger in a way that creates frustration and disharmony. This kind of anger may be displayed in quiet nonparticipation or behind-the-scenes sabotage. Usually people using passive-aggressive anger have concluded they cannot win an argument with open force, so they become evasive and unapproachable instead. Here are some characteristics of passive-aggressive anger:

- ignoring people or tuning others out
- chronic forgetfulness or not following through on promises
- laziness and procrastination
- unreliability in following through on tasks
- telling others what they want to hear with no intention of doing what is said
- appearing cooperative but being uncooperative behind the scenes
- chronic tardiness; waiting until the last minute to get things done
- becoming silent in conflict

Because passive-aggressive people assume that voicing their convictions assertively will result in pain, their anger is driven by fear and a craving for power. They gain control in relationships through quiet stubbornness only to later deny that that was their goal.

## Turning Anger into Insight

When anger wells up, take the time to ask yourself why this particular behavior makes you angry. Why does it push your buttons? You may find that your anger will highlight some issues you need to deal with in your own life. For example, are you angry because you feel your child's behavior reflects badly on you? Some of us fear that others will judge us as bad parents if our child misbehaves. Is your child's behavior embarrassing or not living up to your expectations? As you reflect, you may find that some of your identity is related to being the parent of the "overachieving child." Is your child's failure in some area bringing up old feelings from your childhood? Take a hard look inside, pray, and honestly evaluate the situations that make you angry to see if you are burdening your child by expecting him or her to validate you. This is one of the more difficult aspects of self-exploration because we want so badly to rationalize our behavior. But recognizing when we are projecting our needs onto our kids is essential if we want to develop an empathetic relationship that allows us to walk alongside them through their experiences.

## Love Withdrawal

One thing we particularly want to avoid, especially when expressing our anger, is the child's perception that we are withdrawing from them emotionally or creating a break in the relationship. This is a frightening message to a child, and it can be delivered both verbally and nonverbally through aggressive statements or actions or through a subtle withdrawal of warmth, approval, and emotional presence. It might even take the form of a sigh or long-suffering look.

The sense that a parent is withdrawing his love puts the child in a very difficult predicament. Wanting a secure bond with his parents, the child may try several strategies. One is to try to win the parents' approval by compulsively striving for achievement, being perfect, or taking care of the parents. Another strategy is to withdraw and never be a burden or provoke the parents' anger. The last strategy is to resort to outright rebellion. Some kids misbehave because getting some attention—even negative attention—is better than nothing at all. Failing grades, getting kicked off a team, or getting fired from a job are all passive-aggressive ways that kids can fight back against parents who threaten their bonding.

Research has shown that children who believe a parent is withdrawing his or her love as a consequence for bad behavior are more prone to depression, anxiety disorders, suppressed anger, shame, and feelings of being incompetent and unworthy of being loved.[17] Furthermore, the coping styles they adopt to win their parent's attention or affection often become pervasive patterns of relating to others that last throughout their adult life.[18]

Think back to your own childhood. Perhaps you adopted one of these coping styles—trying to be perfect, denying your needs, withdrawing, or rebelling—in response to the way you were raised. What was once a necessary way to maintain a sense of attachment may now be causing problems in your relationships and your parenting. The first step toward healthier interactions is to ask God to reveal these patterns. The second step is to recognize and face our unhealthy coping mechanisms and to start making better choices.

## Healthy Anger

So what does healthy anger look like? Healthy anger considers your own value, needs, and convictions while also respecting the other person's value, feelings, and thoughts. It recognizes that some injustice has occurred that has inspired your anger but that your response will not compound the problem. If you want to be treated with dignity, you must treat others with dignity even when you are angry. Here are some characteristics of healthy anger:

- speaking confidently but remaining calm
- being specific about your unmet needs
- knowing when to say no and being firm in that decision
- talking about difficult issues in a respectful way
- doing what is right despite opposition
- sticking to good plans instead of being talked into less wise decisions
- clearly explaining what you can and cannot do
- setting boundaries
- following through with consequences when necessary
- addressing problems quickly as opposed to letting them simmer

Ideally, families are a safe haven where these life lessons can be learned in an environment filled with unconditional love and truth. When parents encourage and demonstrate the godly expression of emotions—including anger—they lay the groundwork for their children to develop healthy ways to handle anger in other relationships. With this goal in mind, the following are some practical ways we can express our anger without being disrespectful to our children.

## Be Authentic

Sometimes, we go to great lengths to mask our angry feelings, but our kids usually pick up on suppressed anger. This can be confusing to our children because it is a mixed message. Just as we need to accept our children's feelings, we need to accept ours as well. What we suggest is not an unbridled release of emotions but the willingness to recognize how we feel and communicate it respectfully to our kids. When we do, we are less likely to harbor resentment and end up with our anger exploding in a disrespectful way. For example, let's say you come home from the grocery store and call out for your kids to help. As you start to put the groceries away, you notice no one has moved. Instead of finishing the job yourself or giving them an icy stare, what if you said, "When I ask for help and no one moves, I feel resentful"? You may need to deliver consequences. But when you're honest about your feelings, you give your kids an opportunity to take another person's concerns into consideration.

## Communicating Anger through "I" Messages

When we're angry, it can be tempting to make statements that devalue our children's character, ability, or personality. "You are so lazy!" is an example. Sentences that start with "You are ..." are likely to sound like attacks or insults. Instead, start the sentence with "When I ..." followed by a description of what you see and feel. For example, "When I ask you over and over again to stop playing the game and I'm ignored, I get very frustrated!" Or "When I see the ice cream left out, I'm angry that it is going to waste."

## Being Initiators instead of Reactors

A key to delivering consequences is to recognize when children's behavior is dictating our responses. Most of us desire respect, appreciation, and understanding. When our kids get upset, argue, or withdraw, it can expose our insecurities. In a flash, we may blow up, despite our good intentions. As parents, it's important to recognize when we are reacting rather than initiating. We must realize we have a choice. We can choose to display our anger in negative ways (reactors), or we can exercise emotional control—regardless of how our children behave (initiators). Overcoming our sinful tendencies takes planning, practice, and a commitment to being more Christlike. Knowing our areas of weakness will help us stay calm, use reflective listening, and wait until we have cooled off before delivering a consequence.

## MICHELLE'S BOX

Chris and I were reminded of the importance of being an initiator rather than a reactor when Bob was nineteen. One of the rules in our house was that before leaving in the morning, you make your bed, put dirty dishes into the dishwasher, and put all dirty clothes in the hamper. At the time, this was a new rule and it took a little while for Bob to adjust. When he left some of his dishes out, we decided the consequence would be an extra chore: folding clothes. When he got home late that night, we gave him the choice of folding the clothes then or folding them in the morning. Not surprisingly, he chose the morning.

The next day, he was running late and scrambling to get out the door. Because he still hadn't done the extra folding, I said, "Feel free to go to work as soon as this folding is done."

He replied, "Why can't I fold them this afternoon? Why does it matter so much to you? If I fold them now, I'll be late for work!"

I said, "I'm sorry you feel like I'm being unfair. However, I still need you to do the folding."

Angrily, he folded he clothes. This was tough for me. He hurt my feelings. I felt like he blamed me for his procrastination. Everything in me wanted to lash out and remind him that he knew the rules, he could have done it the night before, but *he* chose to leave it until morning. But I resisted the urge to respond in the heat of the moment with an angry verbal defense. Instead, I left the room to talk with Chris and admitted to him that I was mad and trying hard not to blow it. The encouraging support of a spouse can be a great asset in these situations!

A few minutes later, after finishing the folding, Bob came into the room and said sheepishly, "I can't find my car keys to get to work. Will you help me find them?"

Because he had just demonstrated a really bad attitude, I calmly said, "Normally, I'd be happy to help you find your keys. But I'm not inclined to do favors for people who treat me the way you did this morning."

He stormed out of the room. When he still couldn't find his keys, he asked if he could borrow one of our cars.

"No, that really won't work for us today. Sorry," Chris and I answered.

He eventually talked his brother into loaning him his car. Then, something amazing happened. As he walked out the door, he cheerfully said, "Bye, Mom," as though nothing had occurred.

We got a call from him a few minutes later asking what he could do for us if we helped him find his missing keys. The sense of entitlement had vanished and he was in problem-solving mode—right where we wanted him to be. We offered to look for the keys if he would bring home a couple of coffees for us after work. He agreed, and after an extensive search, we found the keys under a seat cushion. He brought us the coffees and learned several lessons about time management, delayed gratification, respect for others, and having the humility necessary to repent and restore a relationship after conflict.

I learned that consequences with empathy really do work, and sometimes, the most loving thing I can do doesn't feel very loving. The situation could have turned out much differently if I had followed my initial reaction, which was aggressive anger. Maintaining a calm, empathetic attitude kept the focus on his behavior and helped him learn something from the process.

## Take Your Time

Sometimes, a natural consequence isn't obvious and you don't know what to do. Other times, your anger may make it difficult to deliver consequences with empathy in the heat of the moment. In these instances, delaying consequences is a good idea. There's nothing wrong with waiting until you've had some time to cool off, considered possible consequences, or talked with your spouse or a close friend. In fact, sometimes waiting can be more effective than delivering a consequence on the spot because it gives your child a little time to think about the situation. He likely will do some self-exploration, which can enhance the learning process.

Even if you decide to delay giving a consequence, make sure you acknowledge the poor choice immediately. You want your children to learn to recognize when a boundary has been crossed. Bringing it to their attention right away will help them become more adept at recognizing poor choices in the future and to understand why a consequence is necessary. If you don't acknowledge the poor choice when it happens, the children may have trouble remembering the event later or they may remember the circumstances differently. Recognizing a poor choice right away eliminates confusion.

You can say something like "That wasn't a good choice. I'm going to have to get back to you on a consequence." The child is alerted that a boundary has been crossed and that a consequence will be delivered later. He has some time to think about why and what he did. The next step is to come up with the best natural and reasonable consequence you can muster.

Although it is often helpful to delay giving a consequence, be sure not to wait too long before you follow through. This is especially true with small children because they have a shorter attention span and the learning opportunity passes more quickly. For this reason, we don't recommend delaying consequences for kids who are under two or three years old.

## Don't Expect Appreciation

Nobody likes getting consequences for their poor choices. Be honest. After you get a speeding ticket, do you vent your frustration to a friend or family member, even when you deserved it? When you arrive two minutes after the dry cleaner closed and you can't pick up your clothes, how do you respond? Most people are frustrated when they face consequences, and our kids are no different. Rather than expecting immediate capitulation, remorse, and repentance from our kids, we should brace ourselves for objections. Knowing this in advance will help you respond to these objections with empathy rather than unhealthy anger, frustration, or sarcasm.

## Don't Try to "Sell" the Logic of Your Consequences

When kids object to a consequence, many parents feel the need to justify their actions. While it's appropriate to explain the reason for a consequence in one or two sentences (otherwise, kids may not know why the behavior is wrong), sometimes we go into a long discourse of why the consequence is deserved. We don't need to sell the legitimacy of our decision. When we respond to our kids' objections with attempts at persuasion, many of them see this as a lack of conviction on our part and an invitation to debate the consequences. For some kids, arguing becomes a way of controlling the situation and distracting the focus from their poor choice.

When kids argue about a consequence that you have already sufficiently explained, don't take the bait! Short responses, such as "I can see you're disappointed" or even just an *oh* or a *mm-hmm* sometimes allow the conflict to fizzle out. But if the arguing persists, it's best to opt out of the exchange. We've known kids who follow their parents from room to room in an effort to keep the debate going. If that happens, you might turn and ask a question that reminds them of the choice they made. "Do you think it would be a good or a bad idea for you to keep arguing about this?" If they choose to persist, additional consequences must be given.

Instead of debating the consequences, you can empathize with your kids that no one likes consequences. Tell them how sorry you feel for their situation. Of course, you won't change or forego the consequence. But you can let them know you understand it's not going to be much fun. Try listening and reflecting their feelings back to them. "Wow, it sounds like you really don't want to do that. You seem frustrated." Or say, "You're angrier than usual about this. Would you like to talk about it?" Sometimes, empathy and reflective listening can provide the sense of safety and security needed for your child to open up the deeper issues that led him or her to make the poor choice in the first place.

## Objecting versus Disrespect

Disrespect is a different issue than objecting. The difference is that an objection is about a *situation*—the choice the child made that results in a consequence he doesn't like. Disrespect is about a *person*—the child makes a person the target of his words or actions. For example, if the consequence for leaving dirty clothes on the floor is to fold and put away clean clothes, your child might say he hates folding clothes and doesn't see why he can't just wear them with wrinkles. That's an objection. You can counter by empathizing that you understand he doesn't see the purpose of folding clothes, but that nevertheless you prefer to have them folded.

When the objection turns into a personal attack, such as "You are a neat freak and must be crazy to make a kid do this kind of pointless work," the objection has crossed the line into disrespect. At that point, the central issue isn't about the situation (folding clothes) but about a person (you). We are aware of the gray area between objecting and disrespect that will require a judgment call on your part. When in doubt, we strongly recommend using a positive approach to teach better communication skills by asking the child, "Can you think of a more respectful way to say that?" In this way, you can address the situation even as you give them an opportunity to rephrase their statements more respectfully.

If they continue in their disrespectful attack, we suggest you stop, let a little silence pass, and then quietly say, "I feel very disrespected when you talk to me that way." Pausing and pointing out disrespect calmly allows the lesson to sink in. You can deliver the consequence right away or delay it, but make sure you acknowledge disrespect immediately. That will help the child better understand when he or she is being disrespectful in the future.

Sometimes, children are disrespectful in more passive ways, such as refusing to cooperate, withdrawing, or giving you the silent treatment. Most often, children act this way because they do not expect their parents to listen to their concerns. Sensing that they do not have a way to express their frustrations without receiving critical or judgmental responses, they resort to more passive forms of communication. If this characterizes your child, take some time to consider how you usually respond. Do you get your feelings hurt easily and immediately respond in a defensive way? Are you willing to try to see the situation from your child's point of view even when you disagree with him?

When our children are critical of us, it can hit at the core of our identity. When we feel that we are being mischaracterized by our children, we may think, *After all I've done for them! I can't believe they are so unappreciative!* This often causes us to point out their faults and defend our actions. It takes an incredible amount of self-control to put these reactions on hold and focus on listening to what is going on inside your child. But it is an effort that will ultimately lead to closer relationships and more authentic communication.

Keep in mind that maintaining your composure in these situations is about as Christlike as you can get. Although he was the Son of God, Jesus humbled Himself by coming to earth and living among us! He could have exercised His divine authority by simply demanding that we obey, but He chose *relationship* instead. If you struggle to extend empathy to your kids, consider this: Jesus literally walked in our shoes. "For we do not have a high priest who is unable to sympathize with our weaknesses, but one who in every respect has been tempted as we are, yet without sin. Let us then with confidence draw near to the throne of grace, that we may receive mercy and find grace to help in time of need" (Heb. 4:15,16). Jesus experienced the ultimate in disrespect as He was crucified, yet He was able to say, "Father, forgive them, for they do not know what they are doing" (Luke 23:34). This is the mind-set we want to adopt when our children are disrespectful to us.

## Bringing It Home

Consequences are much more effective when we deliver them well. This may require you to delay consequences until you have had time to cool off and come up with a good lesson. A delay gives your child time to sit and think about what happened and hopefully make better choices in the future.

One of the biggest obstacles to empathetic delivery of consequences is poorly expressed anger. Anger can be a productive emotion when it motivates us to address sin, but too often our anger is expressed in unhealthy ways through suppression, aggression, or passive aggression. The goal of healthy, assertive anger is to voice our convictions in a way that preserves our dignity and the dignity of our kids. We can do this by calmly giving our children reasonable consequences instead of nagging, yelling, or giving them the silent treatment.

When we give consequences with empathy, most kids will not be thrilled to be on the receiving end. Allow room for them to express their objections in a respectful way, but don't get drawn into a debate or try to sell them on the legitimacy of your decision. Most of all, be careful not to withdraw from your children emotionally or withhold your love as a consequence. This can lead to children adopting lifelong unhealthy coping patterns.

Giving consequences can be challenging, but they can also be opportunities to understand our kids and ourselves better. Responding to our kids' poor decisions in a godly way will require us to dig deeper. When we look at the situation from their perspective, we can learn a lot about the unique way our children are made as well as the challenges they are facing. We will also learn a lot about ourselves—the issues that push our buttons and the unhealthy ways we tend to respond. Although it may take you out of your comfort zone, allow God to use these times to uncover the motivations of your heart and motivate you to grow more like Him.

# CHAPTER 14

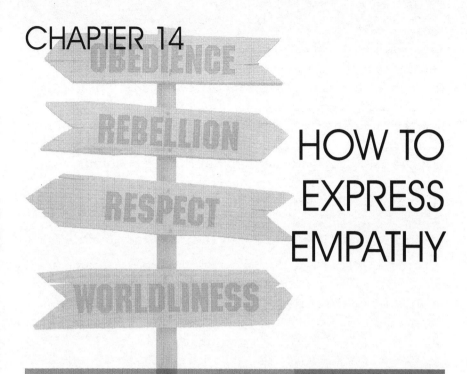

# HOW TO EXPRESS EMPATHY

A family came to our office for counseling. They had two boys who were extremely anxious, and their anxiety was causing problems for them socially and academically. After talking with the parents, it became clear the dad was a dictator style of parent. As we discussed the importance of empathy, he admitted being reluctant to take that approach because he thought empathy would breed entitlement. "They just need clear direction and correction," he said.

Michelle's heart ached for the boys. They didn't need direction and correction as much as they needed a dad who would listen when they talked about their struggles and their victories. It was clear they wanted their dad to be interested in who they were and what made them tick.

Several months passed before they came back, but when they did, it was clear from the moment they walked into the office that something was different. The dad looked more relaxed and less on edge. The boys were in great spirits. Michelle asked the dad how things were going and he said, "Great!" He shared that he had finally decided to try some of our parenting suggestions—particularly empathy. When his son played poorly in a basketball game, instead of pointing out where he could improve, he asked his son, "What did you think of the game?" and then listened. The dad said, "I started to realize that my boys might have a different perspective on things, and that's okay. I was so set on forcing the boys to see my perspective that I missed seeing theirs. Once I made efforts to understand their point of view, things have been much better."

Michelle later spoke to the nine-year-old son alone and it was clear that his anxiety was much better. In particular, she asked him about a habit he had of throwing himself into the wall when he got frustrated. His reply was "Oh, I don't do that anymore."

## Empathy Is the Glue That Holds the Principles Together

After learning about these parenting principles, Michelle and I began giving choices and consequences. But it took us much longer to understand the nature of empathy and how to authentically communicate it to our boys. We discovered it was *the* essential piece of the relationship puzzle. Without empathy, choices can look like a trap, our example can seem like a prideful display, and exploration becomes cross-examination. This truth bears repeating. Empathy is the glue that holds the Parenting by Design principles together. No matter how skilled you become at giving choices or delivering consequences, a real connection with your kids is possible only when you do those things with empathy.

As we mentioned earlier in the book, to be truly empathetic you must enter your child's world and emotions. We know that hearing ideas and viewpoints that are different from your own can evoke many emotions inside of you, and that's why empathy requires maturity and self-control. You must be willing to put aside your fear, pride, anger, and defensiveness and respond to your kids with a desire to get to know them better. Pointing out the fallacies of their reasoning is easier than listening to their experience and feelings from their perspective. But this is the very step that makes a parent a safe person to talk to. If you take the time and effort to learn how to communicate with empathy, we believe your kids will take more risks in telling you what's going on in their world. They desperately want you to know them, but if they don't believe you will hear their perspective, they will probably confide in others that "get" them.

Being empathetic is more difficult if you struggle with issues of your own. If you are pushing your kids to perform so you can feel appreciated, respected, competent, loved, or successful, you will have a difficult time seeing a difficult situation from their perspective. Instead, you will be more interested in getting the behavior you need from them to feel better about yourself. If you can let go of your baggage, give up trying to control your kids, and spend the effort necessary to get to know them, you can reach a deeper understanding of your kids and be the godly parent they deserve.

While this mind-set is essential, we recognize it is very difficult to achieve. Most of us tend to lapse into sarcasm, judgment, condemnation, condescension, and resentment—especially when emotions run high. Ask God to reveal your weaknesses in being empathetic so you and He can deal with them. Involve others too. Insight into your parenting motivations is difficult to attain without a community of other likeminded parents. As in other Christian pursuits, parenting is more effective when you practice it in a loving community that truly cares about each other and speaks the truth in love. If you are transparent and empathetic with other parents, they can help you see how you can approach your kids in a healthier way. When you find yourself lacking in some area, ask God for wisdom. He will provide it for those who ask. (See James 1:5.)

## Expressing Empathy

In this chapter, we look at the nuts and bolts of expressing empathy in a variety of situations. Our parenting model is God. Even though He knew man would rebel over and over, He loved us anyway. When we rebelled, He sent His Son to save us. This picture of unconditional love is best expressed in Romans 5:8, which says, "While we were still sinners, Christ died for us." Jesus came to earth and walked in our shoes. He endured temptation and He felt the pain of rejection, and as a result, He could identify with our condition. If empathy is the ability to enter and see the world from the perspective of another, there is no better demonstration of empathy than Jesus' incarnation.

Our goal is to love our kids as God loves us. When God tells us He will never leave us or forsake us (Heb. 13:5), we understand His love to be unconditional. That's what it means to be part of His family, and that's the model for our family too. Our kids must know that nothing will separate them from our love. No matter what mistakes they make or consequences they must endure, they will never be kicked out of the family. Don't misunderstand this. Consequences are still essential. Unconditional love does not mean rescuing kids from consequences. It means loving them *despite* the consequences. We have a friend who visits her son in prison every other weekend to let him know he is loved, but she does not try to bail him out or make excuses for him because she understands his consequence was deserved.

## Communication 101

Does someone in your life have a communication style that frustrates you? What characterizes this person's interaction with you?

### MICHELLE'S BOX

I have a friend who seems interested in what's going on in my life and will enthusiastically ask me questions. Sometimes, as I start to answer the first question, she asks a second question. Other times, while I'm in the middle of my answer, she interrupts and asks another question or changes the subject. Although her outward demeanor makes it appear that she's interested, I often wonder if she really wants to hear what I have to say.

Another friend of mine tries to solve my problems. Instead of allowing me to express my thoughts and feelings, she immediately makes suggestions and gives advice.

I have a third friend who responds in a way that makes me feel heard and understood. Somehow by talking with her, I can clarify what I feel and think about a situation. I realize now that she uses good communication skills and avoids the roadblocks outlined in this chapter. Guess which of these friends I call when I am struggling.

Being empathetic requires effective communication skills. One of the best things you can do to improve your relationship with your child is to take an honest look at your communication skills. The truth is most of us tend to respond to our kids in ways that are almost guaranteed to create roadblocks to a deeper relationship. This is even more likely when emotions are high. Here is a list of common roadblocks described in the book *People Skills: How to Assert Yourself, Listen to Others, and Resolve Conflicts,* by Robert Bolton:[19]

- Criticizing: "You have no one to blame but yourself."
- Name-calling: "You are so stubborn!"
- Diagnosing: "You are just doing that to irritate me."
- Ordering: "Do your homework right now."
- Threatening: "Stop making that noise right now or I'll ground you."
- Moralizing: "You ought to tell him you're sorry."
- Excessive questioning: "When did it happen? Are you sorry you did it?"
- Advising: "If I were you, I'd ..."
- Diverting: "Don't dwell on it" or "You think you've got it bad. Let me tell you what happened to me."
- Logical argument: "The most reasonable thing would have been not to buy the new car."
- Reassuring: "It will all work out."

These are some of the ways we subtly shut down conversations with our kids, dismiss their feelings, and short-circuit their learning experiences. Instead, let's try to encourage open and honest conversations about the issues. When our kids' emotions cause us anxiety, we might feel the quickest way to stop the pain (theirs and ours) is to avoid the emotions causing it, but that's a lack of empathy. We're told in Scripture to rejoice with those who rejoice and weep with those who weep. (See Rom. 12:15.) Our kids need us to acknowledge their emotions as real and legitimate and to give them the chance to celebrate, grieve, or be upset about the things they are going through. Walking with them through their emotions is a real relationship builder.

## Accept Your Child's Feelings

The first step to communicating empathetically is to accept our children's feelings and perceptions. Again, we don't always realize the subtle ways we deny our kids' feelings. But think about the messages we send when we make statements, such as the following:

- "You have no reason to be upset."
- "It couldn't hurt. It's only a little scratch."
- "How can you be tired? You've hardly done anything."
- "Don't cry. You have lots of other friends."

Unintentionally, these responses say to our kids that the following:

- You don't mean what you say.
- You don't know what you think you know.
- You don't feel what you think you feel.[20]

Responses like these can have profound, long-lasting consequences for kids because they invalidate and confuse their experience. A child whose feelings are denied may begin to doubt or lose touch with those feelings. For example, a child who is told "big boys don't cry" may begin to doubt that others have really hurt him. He also may fail to learn about the limits on what is appropriate behavior, either as a bully or a victim. Over time, these kids may have trouble knowing what they like or dislike, what they value, or what they believe. In addition, they may learn not to expect others to understand or be interested in what they say, furthering the feelings of isolation. And if they don't trust their perceptions when someone does something that makes them feel uncomfortable, they will be vulnerable to people who want to take advantage of them.

Empathy communicates that their feelings—both good and bad—are important. It encourages kids to get in touch with these feelings rather than denying or suppressing them, and it gives them a chance to discuss the feelings with you. They will be better equipped to understand their motivations, to communicate with others in an authentic way, and to trust their instincts when others are pressuring them to do things they don't want to do. In addition, when our children feel they are being heard and understood, they are free to respond more lovingly.

## Listening Is a Skill

When you've decided to empathetically engage with your child's feelings, the next step is to learn how to be the kind of listener who encourages your child to share those feelings. We often assume we are good listeners, but the truth is that being an effective listener is difficult for many people. To be a better listener, it helps to break listening down into separate clusters of skills. In *People Skills*, Bolton outlines three types of listening skills: attending skills, following skills, and reflecting skills.

## *Attending Skills*

*Attending* means giving your physical attention to another person. The right amount of attending is conveyed to our kids through nonverbal cues, such as posture, body language, eye contact, and minimizing distractions. While most of us know these things are important for listening, we often forget to do them. But research shows that 85 percent of communication is nonverbal. Set some time aside to observe how well you attend when you communicate with your children. You might also ask your spouse or friends to weigh in. Ask yourself whether you make a conscious effort to be relaxed and open. Are your arms and legs crossed or uncrossed? Do you lean toward them to show your interest? Are you too close or too far away? Do you make an effort to bend down to their eye level? You are less intimidating when you are at your child's level, so this is especially important for small children.

## *Following Skills*

Do you listen in a way that encourages your kids to be vulnerable and open? Part of being an effective listener is avoiding the roadblocks that derail authentic communication. We communicate empathy and encourage our kids to talk when we employ good "following" skills: door openers, minimal encouragers, infrequent questions, and attentive silence.

The door opener is a nonthreatening invitation to talk. For example, "Looks like things didn't go too well for you today. I've got time if you'd like to talk." This is followed by silence to give your kids a chance to decide if they want to talk and if so what they'd like to say. Compare that response to the parent who sees her kids dragging in from school and says, "Cheer up" or "What's the matter, grumpy?" Both of these comments imply a judgment about behavior and will normally shut your kids down or start a fight.

Minimal encouragers can help you navigate the fine line between being interested and being pushy. They are simple responses that encourage your kids to tell their story in their way. Just a few words can let your children know you are listening without interrupting the flow of the conversation or trying to control it. A skilled listener can communicate empathy through voice and facial expressions even when only one or two words are said. Some examples of minimal encouragers are the following:

- *Mm-hmm ...*
- Tell me more.
- I see.
- For instance ...
- Really?
- Wow!

## MICHELLE'S BOX

I would get so excited to hear all the details about my kids' school day that I would greet them with a barrage of questions as soon as they got in the car. "How was your day? How did your project go? What did you eat for lunch? Do you have any homework?" It hurt my feelings when they gave me one-word answers or didn't seem to want to talk. In fact, that usually made me want to ask more questions! When we started teaching parenting classes, I'll never forget the words of one high school counselor when I asked what advice she would give to parents. She said, "Dads need to get in the game and *moms talk too much!*"

## LEE'S BOX

I encourage parents to avoid being like a bad date when they're talking with their kids by not being overly pushy or eager. You can probably remember being turned off by a date who was a little too determined to get you to like them. The same rationale applies in talking to your kids. If they sense you are overly interested, they often compensate by backing away. When you use minimal encouragers followed by silence, your kids are less likely to feel that you are intruding on their personal space. Give them time to get comfortable and warm up to the conversation. This kind of space is especially important if you want them to share difficult situations and emotions. At the end of the day, you can't make your children be transparent and vulnerable. But giving them some space can make your offer to talk a lot more inviting.

One mom told me that every time she tried to get her teenage son to talk, he said as little as possible and retreated to his room as soon as possible. So she tried something different. After school, she made some snacks and kept quiet. Her son sat down and started to graze, and after a few minutes of silence, he started a conversation. She admitted she wanted to ask tons of questions, but she restrained herself and tried minimal encouragers instead. The result was a conversation about everything that had happened that day and more. This mom was amazed how much more her son shared when it was on his timing rather than hers.

## Reflective Skills

Another key component of empathy is reflective skills. The goal of reflecting is to clarify and amplify your child's experience and emotions without imposing your own opinions and thoughts. When a parent reflects well, he or she restates the facts and feelings the child has communicated in a way that demonstrates understanding. Good reflecting is not simply parroting back what your children have said. Instead, you try to understand how the experience has made them feel. Paraphrasing, reflecting feelings, and reflecting meanings are three ways to be reflective.

A paraphrase focuses on restating the facts being communicated by your child. Examples are "You want me to pick you up at the school at four o'clock?" and "You're spending the night at Janie's house?" We could reduce a significant amount of confusion and miscommunication if we would just take time to paraphrase the facts.

Reflecting feelings involves mirroring back to our child the emotions she is communicating. The key to reflecting emotions is to look for the feeling words expressed by our kids in the conversation or the emotions being communicated through their body language. Examples of reflecting emotions include "That sounds really discouraging," "You seem so angry," and "You look like you're really happy."

A reflected meaning is a succinct response that sums up *both* the feelings and the facts. When we get used to reflecting facts by paraphrasing and reflecting emotions by mirroring feelings, it is easier to put the two together into a reflection of meaning. Some parents find it helpful to use these words: "You *feel* (insert the feeling word) *because* (insert the event or content associated with the feeling)." Here are some examples: "You feel angry because you weren't invited to the party" and "You are really excited that you made the cheerleading squad!" This is a different way of communicating that may feel unnatural at first, but over time, it will get easier to include reflective listening into your own personal style.

Reflective responses give our kids a chance to confirm if we have understood them correctly. We've all played the game where a large group of people gets in a circle and a phrase is quietly given to one person to whisper to the person next to him. This is repeated until the phrase has been passed around the entire circle. We're always amazed at how distorted that phrase becomes while passed from person to person. But that's an example of how important it is to verify that you hear the exact message being conveyed. Reflective responses minimize errors and allow our kids to clarify what they truly meant. An added side benefit is that reflective responses help children process their emotions and become more aware of them.

Helping a child clarify his feelings isn't the same as agreeing with, condoning, or reinforcing the feelings. As parents, we can accept our kids' feelings as we set good boundaries for their behavior. Here are some examples:

"Claire, I know you'd like to gather up a big bunch of flowers and bring them home, but the sign says that flowers can't be picked in the park. I'm so sorry."

"Janie, I know you'd like to bite into every chocolate in the box just to see what's inside. It's so tempting. But what you can do is pick out one piece now and another tomorrow."

"Brad, you're so mad at Eric for breaking your bicycle you'd like to punch him, I know. But tell him with words, not with your fist."

## Four Kinds of Empathy

Why do so many parent-child conflicts end up looking like a baseball manager and umpire shouting at each other—an angry face-to-face confrontation? That's the antithesis of empathy. We want you to see empathy as disengaging from face-to-face confrontations and looking at the issue like two people walking beside each other. When you're facing the same direction, you can face the problem together. The focus is dealing with the issue as a team.

Walking alongside your kids also means you have to put away your agenda and focus on the lessons your child can learn with you by his side. In this chapter and the next, we'll look at four different situations where you can use the communication tools we've discussed to express empathy. The goal is to help you get to know your child and at the same time let him or her know you are respectful of the challenges God gives him to help him grow and mature.

## Empathy for Good Behavior

A lot of parents, particularly dictators, miss the opportunity to show empathy for good behavior because they take it for granted. After all, good behavior is expected, right? Unfortunately that's not how kids—or adults—are wired. Failing to recognize positive behavior can even result in a kid who begins to believe that the only way to get attention is to misbehave. While that kind of attention isn't much fun for the child, at least he knows you see him. Failing to recognize and affirm good behavior can reinforce negative behavior and have long-term detrimental effects.

**Empathy versus praise.** Expressing empathy for positive behavior is very different from simply praising a result. Being empathetic about your child's *experience* is far more valuable. This is an important distinction. How you play the game really *is* more important than who wins or loses. Results can be arbitrary and out of the control of your child, but a good effort is always possible. Being more empathetic about the process than the result tells your child that a good effort is appreciated, and a good result is icing on the cake. When we keep praising results, such as a game-winning goal, our kids can get a skewed impression they are valuable only when they produce that result. That can lead them to focus on external behavior that produces praiseworthy results, no matter what it may take to achieve them. Cheating is a common side effect of a kid who is focused too much on results and not enough on a solid effort.

Jesus taught a lot about the priority of attitude over results.

> Be careful not to do your "acts of righteousness" before men, to be seen by them. If you do, you will have no reward from your Father in heaven. So when you give to the needy, do not announce it with trumpets, as the hypocrites do in the synagogues and on the streets, to be honored by men. I tell you the truth, they have received their reward in full. But when you give to the needy, do not let your left hand know what your right hand is doing, so that your giving may be in secret. Then your Father, who sees what is done in secret, will reward you.
>
> Matthew 6:1–4

Clearly, God considers the effort and the process more important than the outward result. He criticized the Pharisees for neglecting internal holiness and focusing on external behavior by calling them "whitewashed tombs" (Matt. 23:27).

**Describe rather than evaluate.** How can we focus on the process more than the results? By being specific and using words that *describe* rather than words that *evaluate*. Words such as *good, wonderful*, and *brilliant* are vague and can become a subtle pressure on our kids to perform up to our standards. Instead, be specific about the action or attitude you value. For example, instead of making the vague and general evaluation "You are such a nice girl," try saying, "I really appreciated it when you unloaded the dishwasher without being asked."

Describing rather than evaluating also helps our kids clarify and communicate what *they* enjoyed, disliked, or learned from the experience. For example, "You sure seemed to be having fun playing soccer today. Was it as much fun as it seemed?"

## LEE'S BOX

I have a niece who is a talented artist. Seeing a picture she painted, I told her how good I thought her painting was. She responded with, "Oh, Uncle Lee, you always say that." Recognizing that I had not been specific enough, I started to describe elements of the picture that interested me. I asked her how she chose the colors she used, why she picked the subject of the painting, and what inspired the border. As I became more specific, my niece became more animated about her experience. My questions and observations encouraged her to open up, and as a result, I was able to know her better. In that short conversation, she had a chance to reveal a little about her life because I was an empathetic, safe, and interested person to talk to.

**Empathy for mistreatment and failures.** Eventually, every kid will be disappointed by events that were not a result of a poor choice on his or her part. Kids will be bullied or ridiculed, get cut from a team, or find themselves excluded from a clique they really wanted to be a part of. Events like these are traumatic for kids trying to establish their value, competence, or worth, and they will need a safe shoulder to cry on. Empathy in these times will require you to be still, listen, and let your children grieve their loss. Kids need someone who will weep with them while they weep and who will enter their experience for the purpose of listening, reflecting, and offering hope.

Empathy in these situations will require you to bite your lip and be there for your children. You've got to resist the temptation to solve problems, make excuses, or place blame. Let them pour out their emotions while you listen, reflecting those emotions so they will know you're tracking with them. We assume our kids come to us to take their pain away, but that is rarely the case. Kids who are in pain know they are in pain, and they usually don't expect you to take away the pain. More often than not, they want someone to experience the pain with them—a loving parent who shows that he or she understands why it hurts. They need someone who, after sitting through the experience with them, can encourage them from a place of true understanding.

When we try to rescue our kids from their pain, they will often resist and defend their right to feel that way! A parent who jumps straight to fixing a problem sends an implied message to the child that it is not okay to feel that way and that the child needs to move past the pain quickly. That kind of attitude leaves a child feeling dismissed. Isn't that your experience when you complain to someone about some injustice in your life? You feel wronged and want someone to know it, but when the other person tells you it's really no big deal or gives you suggestions for how you ought to go about solving the problem, you feel dismissed. You simply wanted to vent, and ironically, her response has actually *added* to your pain!

For instance, some parents respond to a child's peer group rejection by trying to invite all the cool kids over to make sure their child gets into the clique. What happens? The parent undermines the child's ability to come up with solutions and the child ends up embarrassed and angry with Mom or Dad for butting in. Wouldn't it be better to sit down, listen reflectively, and show her you really care? Let her tell you what hurts and why it hurts, and let the grief come to its natural conclusion. Then you can ask her what she plans to do. If she asks, you can brainstorm some solutions with her.

When we try to fix, solve, excuse, blame, or just try to cheer our kids up without acknowledging their pain, that is usually because *we* are anxious and we want the pain to go away. But God often uses painful experiences to help us grow and mature. Trying to cover it up deprives our kids of the learning opportunity. What they really need from us is to acknowledge and understand what they're going through and to let them know the situation isn't hopeless.

## Empathy for Pain You Have Caused

Inevitably, you will do something to hurt your kids. You'll miss a game or a performance, you'll say something you shouldn't in anger or impatience, or you'll dismiss their feelings. When that happens, you'll have to step up and admit you made a mistake. That will require an extra helping of humility.

But this is part of your example to your kids, one of the three E's we talked about in chapter 4. You set a powerful example when you say, "You know when I rolled my eyes at your comment? That was wrong and I want to apologize." You will not believe how influential that message is for your kids. They need to know you're not above the rules, and that you are humble enough to confess, repent, and seek forgiveness from *them*.

Here are some tips on dealing with the pain you cause: Be specific when you confess. Don't just say you haven't been a very good parent. Instead, refer to the particular action or attitude you regret. For example, "I was wrong when I was sarcastic about your grades. I'm sorry for that." After you've apologized specifically about the way you caused your child pain, stop and listen. Some kids may do a little scolding, while others will be quick to let you off the hook. Either response is fine so long as it doesn't become disrespectful. The key is that you want your child to know you really do care about the issue and you are not simply going through the motions. Then ask forgiveness. This communicates that you love your child enough to value his or her forgiveness.

When a parent feels he is above apologizing to his kids, or that humble repentance will somehow detract from his position of authority, there's a problem. That's a classic authoritarian position, and it does not inspire your kids to heartfelt obedience. They will conclude that you believe the rules don't apply to you. That is a confusing message. A child brought up in an environment like that can't wait to be an adult when the rules won't apply to *him*. If you wonder how these kinds of parenting traits are passed from generation to generation, look no farther than the Bible. In 2 Samuel 13:24–18:33, David fails to discipline his son Amnon for the rape of his sister Tamar. Frustrated and angry at his father's lack of action, David's other son Absalom decides he will have to defend his sister's honor. Taking matters into his own hands, Absalom kills Amnon and flees Jerusalem for three years. David has Absalom brought back to Jerusalem, but he refuses to see him and he fails to acknowledge his own contribution to the situation. Eventually, Absalom leads a rebellion that temporarily costs David his throne and ends with Absalom losing his life.

As our children shift from dependence on us to reliance on God, they will realize we aren't perfect. We must show them that the rules apply to everyone and that those who harm others are expected to confess, repent, and ask forgiveness. Ideally, they will do the same when they harm others.

## Bringing It Home

In this chapter, we covered the nature of empathy, the communication skills necessary to convey empathy and the process of giving empathy when our child makes positive choices, mistreatments and failures, and when we have caused them pain. But what about extending empathy when our children are disrespectful or misbehave? How can we be empathetic when we address poor behavior? No doubt about it, being empathetic in these situations is a lot more challenging. But when we keep our end goal in mind—honoring God by treating our children in a respectful way—we discover that conflict can be an opportunity to know and connect to our kids on a deeper level. In the next chapter, we will offer tools for handling conflict in a productive and respectful way.

# CHAPTER 15

OBEDIENCE

REBELLION

RESPECT

CONFLICT!

WORLDLINESS

A mother who was just learning how to express empathy shared a story about her son. He was in seventh grade and one morning came down the stairs yelling because his pants were too short. He screamed at his mother, "How could this happen? Why don't I have any pants that fit?" Initially, the mom took the bait and launched into a shouting match, telling him that his pants weren't *that* short and insisting no one would notice. In response, the son declared, "I'm not going to school!" Mom recognized the path the argument was taking and decided to respond in a different way—with empathy.

Instead of escalating the conflict, she tried reflection. "Wow! It sounds like you're really upset about your pants! You're so upset you don't even want to go to school. Tell me what's going on." Confused by the mom's unexpected response and her interest in his situation, the boy thought a little and then hesitantly told her that some boys at school had teased him about how tall and awkward he had gotten in the last several months. He knew that going to school with pants that were too short would ignite the same teasing and make him feel like an outcast. The real issue wasn't his pants. It was his fear that he didn't fit in with his peers.

The mom had correctly sensed something deeper was at play than the surface issue of pants that were too short. The son's anger was way too intense for what seemed to be a small problem. That alerted her that she needed to ask some open-ended questions to uncover the real underlying issue. Using empathy and reflective listening, she discovered what was at the core of the argument. When this mom used conflict as a way to know her son better, he let her in on his struggle.

After brainstorming possible solutions for the short pants, the son chose to take the hem out of his pants, adding an extra inch to the length and making them look acceptable. When they got to school, he thanked her for her help as he got out of the car. The mom knew she had made a breakthrough in their relationship, but she also knew she couldn't forget about consequences. She said, "No problem. I was happy to help. And John, I know you were upset, but there has to be a consequence for yelling at me this morning. We'll talk about that later. Have a great day."

## Empathy for Poor Behavior

When kids are disrespectful, disobey, or make poor choices, empathy is often the last thing on our minds. These are the times when our unconditional love is really put to the test. This is the fourth type of empathy. As parents, our goal ought to be to address the issue without lapsing into unhealthy expressions of anger. (See Eph. 4:26.) We looked at anger in chapter 14 and gave suggestions for being empathetic while delivering consequences. Now let's look at how we can be empathetic as we deal with the conflict that often results when confronting a child's bad behavior.

## Conflict Is an Opportunity

When we address our children's poor choices, they tend to get defensive and angry. This usually causes us to respond with our own anger as we defend our position and tell them why their behavior was wrong. We often end up in a heated debate about the facts that surrounded their poor decision (in the story above, the length of the pants), but when we address the facts *before* we address our children's *emotions*, the conflict usually escalates. We end up arguing about something that is only the tip of the iceberg—not the real issue causing the emotional eruption. There are a couple of reasons why this is the case.

The first reason is biological. When feelings run high, rational problem solving is very difficult. Emotional arousal turns us into people who are no longer calm. When we are angry or fearful, our adrenaline flows faster and our strength increases by about 20 percent. The liver, pumping sugar into the bloodstream, demands more oxygen from the heart and lungs. The veins become enlarged and the brain centers where thinking takes place do not perform nearly as well. The blood supply in the problem-solving part of the brain is severely decreased because, under stress, a greater portion of blood is diverted to the body's extremities. These physical reactions not only make it difficult to remain calm and empathetic, they make it harder to think through the conflict in a rational way.[21] On the other hand, when we let our children know that their thoughts and feelings have been heard, these physical symptoms often subside. This is one reason why it is helpful to take a break from conflict. This gives you and your child time to cool off before responding.

The second reason we end up arguing about the surface facts rather than the deeper issues is that we fail to understand the dynamics of conflict. The truth is that we will be much more effective in resolving conflict when we learn to recognize what is going on inside our children and ourselves rather than just arguing about the surface issues. But this requires contemplation and insight, and a good amount of empathy. By taking the lead and extending empathy to our kids first, we allow them the opportunity to calm down and process the powerful emotions behind the facts. When we handle emotions with respect, we encourage our kids to think before reacting and to be more vulnerable. Ironically, the strong emotions that make conflict so daunting can actually be a doorway to connect with our kids on a deeper, more meaningful level. Making the most of this opportunity requires a willingness to acknowledge their emotions in an empathetic way.

## Identity Issues Drive Conflict

Where do these strong emotions come from? What is really at the bottom of the conflicts you have with your kids? Why do we get into heated arguments over some of the most inconsequential and mundane things? As you might have gathered, we believe most arguments aren't really about the facts of the situation. Instead, they are a product of a perceived challenge to the basic human desires to feel competent, loveable, and worthy. We call these identity issues because they challenge a person's self-concept at the deepest level. When strong emotions pop up, there is probably an identity issue at play—either for our child or us. While we will often argue about the facts until the cows come home, we won't uncover the identity issue at the root of the conflict unless we learn to look for it and provide a secure environment for our kids to share their vulnerable feelings. Remember the boy in the opening paragraph? He and his mother could have argued for hours about whether his pants were really too short without ever getting to the real identity issue—his fear of rejection by his peers.

As parents, we must put our own identity issues on hold and muster up empathy in these challenging situations so our kids will feel safe enough to explore the identity issues fueling their emotions. We will still have to give consequences for poor behavior, but we can give them in a way that communicates understanding, respect, and love. And we'll have a great opportunity to talk with them about their true identity, that they are the unconditionally loved, accepted, and valued children of a heavenly Father who loved them so much that He sent His Son to die on a cross to have a relationship with them.

## Facts, Emotions, and Identity

Most arguments include three elements: the facts of the situation, the emotions that arise from the situation, and the identity issues that fuel the emotional response. Because identity issues are harder to uncover—especially in the midst of conflict—we tend to get stuck at the fact level of a conflict. We may angrily interrogate our child in an effort to get to the bottom of the facts. "Who were you with? Why didn't you call?" When their responses are less than satisfactory, we argue about the discrepancies in their story or criticize their attitude. Arguing about the facts is a lot easier than empathetically uncovering the identity issues behind the emotions. When we are unaware of the existence of these issues or try to uncover them in an intimidating way, we usually end up embroiled in a heated factual argument that rarely solves anything and leaves your children feeling misunderstood and unknown, even if they don't know exactly why.

Our proposal is that you change the way you think about conflict by treating it as an opportunity to better know your children. When you get what looks like an overblown emotional response to a minor problem, you have most likely stumbled on an identity issue that gives you an opportunity to connect with your child. You can discover what makes your child tick and point him or her toward the only real solution for identity issues—the unconditional love and acceptance of God.

Remember strong emotions are a signal that an identity issue is in play. Make a mental note when your child overreacts that there is probably much more going on than what meets the eye. Even when you respond with empathy, your child may not let you in on what is really going on inside of him, so it may be necessary to wait until a later time to try some exploration. You may have to issue some consequences for the poor behavior in the meantime, but you will know that when things calm down, you can try approaching them again. They will be more likely to respond to your empathetic overtures.

Conflict can point us to the most significant issues in our children's lives, and that is why it is one of the best ways to know your kids at the deepest level. But it takes a strong commitment on the parents' part to understand and deal with their own identity issues first so that they can concentrate on the kids' issues when they arise. Parenting by Design has an audio called *Understanding Conflict with Your Kids,* which is available on the website, that digs into this concept.

## Conflict Resolution Skills

In this rest of this chapter, we will provide practical tools for maximizing the opportunities offered by conflict and for keeping emotions from escalating out of control. Keep in mind that we are not saying you should ignore poor behavior in the process. As parents, we are called to address our children's poor behavior with empathy *and* good consequences. It would not be good parenting to ignore the lessons God will teach your children through the consequences you deliver. What we are suggesting is that you have an additional opportunity to use the experience of conflict to learn more about your kids.

No one enjoys being confronted about his or her actions. Because emotions run high and kids are likely to get angry when they are caught in sin, we can fall into the trap of meeting a child's angry or defensive response with an angry and defensive response of our own. Unless we keep our eye on the prize—a deeper relationship with our kids—we can get drawn into a debate or overpower our kids with heavy-handed authority. We may win the battle but lose the war, costing us an opportunity to establish a meaningful, authentic, and respectful relationship with our children.

Let's look at a couple of ways to maintain our composure while we deal with conflict over poor behavior.

## Assertion Statements

Having a guide on how to express our feelings respectfully can be helpful so that we can be proactive instead of reactive. We suggest that before you confront your children about bad behavior, think about how you can provide a nonjudgmental description of the behavior that needs to be changed, a description of your feelings, and the resulting effect on you of your child's action.[22] Some parents find it helpful to use these words: *"When you ...* (describe the problem behavior), *I feel ...* (describe your feelings), *because ...* (state the effect on you of your child's action)."

Let's look at each of these parts in greater depth.

### *Nonjudgmental Description of the Behavior*

When describing a problem behavior, being specific is important. When you use vague language, your point can be missed. Saying, "When you don't do your part around the house ..." is too fuzzy and confusing. "When you don't shovel the snow in the driveway before going to school ..." is much clearer. When you are specific in your language, your child knows the exact behavior that needs to be addressed.

Although you may think you know the intentions of your child, it is important to describe only observable behaviors. In other words, do not make assumptions about the motives or attitudes behind your child's behavior. For example, "When you were quiet during dinner ..." will be more productive and respectful than saying, "When you were so bored that you didn't talk to anyone during dinner ..." When you make assumptions, you run the risk of being wrong and alienating your child.

In your statements, avoid using sarcasm, exaggerations, and generalizations. These are sure to shut down meaningful communication, as will words that convey absolutes, such as *always* and *never* (e.g., "You never pick up after yourself!"). Sometimes, we use absolutes to emphasize our point, but if our kids think we are exaggerating, they will be less likely to listen to what we have to say.[23] If your child happens to be a little lawyer, you can end up in an extended argument about the exceptions to your absolutes. "I washed the dishes once last month!"

Finally, be brief in your statements. While it can feel good to vent by going into a lengthy discourse about the problem behavior and the resulting effects, your kids will generally tune you out after a few sentences and be less likely to focus on the real issue. Make your description as brief as possible and focus on only one behavior at a time.

### Disclose Your Feelings

This part of the assertion statement tells your kids how you feel about their behavior. But this requires that you properly identify your feelings—a task that is difficult for some people. Here are some examples: "When you borrow my car and don't refill the gas tank, I feel *unfairly treated*." "When you borrow my tools and leave them out in the rain, I feel *annoyed*." It's important to be honest, so don't substitute one emotion for another. For example, some people are more comfortable saying they are sad when what they are really feeling is anger.

### The Effect of the Child's Actions

A child is more likely to receive our message if we can identify the concrete and tangible effects of his or her actions. Using the example above, you might say, "When you borrow my car and don't refill the gas tank, I feel unfairly treated because *I have to pay to fill it up.*" Interestingly, as we identify the effect of our children's actions, we sometimes realize we have overstepped our boundaries and micromanaged their lives. For instance, a mom who doesn't like her daughter's hairstyle might say, "When you wear your hair that way, I feel frustrated because ..." The mom must consider why exactly she is frustrated. Is the reason a legitimate concern or a self-centered preference?

We know a parent who objected to her son's scraggly beard. Each time she saw her son, she couldn't help but bring it up by saying, "You really need to trim that beard" or "You look so handsome when you shave." Before long, she noticed that every time she brought it up, his shoulders slumped and he walked away. If she had spent some time considering what effect his scraggly beard had on her, she might have realized she wanted to control something that wasn't really that important.

## LEE'S BOX

A lot of parents end up in my office because they have taken over some task that really should have been left to their children. As you can imagine, this almost always leads to conflict. In one session, I talked to a mother who struggled to find a summer internship job for her daughter. She was upset because her daughter wouldn't lift a finger to help. The more the mom tried to involve the daughter, the less engaged the daughter became.

During one extra frustrating day, the mom exploded. She yelled at the daughter for her lack of ambition and laziness. She complained about all the time and effort she had put into finding a great summer internship for her daughter. She criticized the daughter's lack of appreciation. When the daughter couldn't take it anymore, she yelled back, "I never asked you to do anything! When you got involved, it was *your* job search, not mine!"

The daughter's response hit the mark because Mom stopped in midsentence. She thought about it and realized she *had* taken over the search. It *had* become her search. But why? The mom realized her identity was being threatened through her daughter's lack of initiative. She was comparing her daughter with the other kids who had gotten good internships. She was upset that both she and her daughter would both look bad when they couldn't report to everybody that the daughter worked at a prestigious company. The conflict wasn't about jobs; it was about whether the daughter was competent and a good reflection on the mom, and whether the mom was a good mother who took care of her family.

Although it was going to be tough on her, the mom realized it would be far better for their relationship if she allowed her daughter to own the process—and the resulting consequences.

196

Sometimes, your child's behavior will have a negative impact on your relationship.[24] In these situations, you need to identify *how* your relationship is affected. For example, a message you might send to a child who has told a lie could be this: "When you say you are at school but you're really at the mall, I feel angry and sad because *I can't trust you to be honest with me.*"

After making an assertion statement, try to be as quiet as possible. Silence allows your children to think about what you said or to say whatever is on their mind. More likely than not, your child will respond in a defensive way. This may be in the form of an excuse, a counterattack on you, or withdrawing.[25] But when we are prepared for a defensive response, we are less likely to escalate the situation with our own defensiveness.

Instead of justifying your statement or becoming aggressive, try shifting gears and listening reflectively to the defensive response.[26] This accomplishes several things. First, it helps reduce your child's defensiveness. When we reflect their responses back to them with respect, the defensiveness subsides. The vicious cycle of increasing defensiveness is broken and constructive conversation can begin. You cannot overestimate the power of empathy in the face of defensiveness!

## Repeat the Process

Repeating this process several times—by reasserting your statement and reflecting the defensive response—may be necessary. If so, send your message again and follow with silence. You probably will get another defensive response, but be patient. Switching between being assertive and reflecting takes a lot of maturity. It typically takes several rounds of delivering a message and reflecting the defensive response back before discussing possible solutions. However, when you reflect their thoughts and feelings, you lay a foundation of security and respect. In the process, your child is much more likely to share the deeper issues that led to the problem behavior in the first place. Addressing problem behaviors as we extend empathy is the essence of speaking the truth in love.

## Problem Solving

When you and your child have each been heard by the other, you are ready to solve the problem. The best way to get your kids invested in making a solution happen is to engage them in the problem-solving process. An excellent way to do this is through collaborative problem solving.

Collaborative problem solving can be used for general disagreements; it isn't limited to addressing problem behaviors. It is also a great tool for helping kids develop the skills they will need as adults, including decision-making, problem-solving, and social skills.

We have summarized below many of the concepts presented in the book *Treating Explosive Kids: The Collaborative Problem-Solving Approach,* by Ross W. Greene and J. Stuart Ablon. They describe three components of collaborative problem solving.

1. empathy
2. defining the problem
3. inviting the child to brainstorm solutions

### Step 1: Empathy

The first step in collaborative problem solving is—what else?—empathy! Your empathy will help your child communicate his or her feelings and concerns. With any disagreement, it is important to provide a way for our children to describe the problem from their perspective. A good way to facilitate this process is by using words like "I've noticed that ..." For instance, if your child hasn't been completing his or her homework, you could say, "I've noticed that homework has been a struggle lately. What's up?" Be sure your tone is not condemning or accusatory. The truth is there are a myriad of things that might be interfering with homework completion. Don't assume you know the source of the problem. In this case, your child might respond that the homework is too difficult, he's too tired, or there's too much noise in the house. These are problems that can be addressed. To solve the problem, it is important to define the child's concern as *specifically* as possible.

Sometimes, kids will make bold pronouncements, such as "I'm not taking my medicine" or "Nobody likes me." Help your child be more specific by offering a reflective response. For example, "You're not taking your medicine. What's up?" Answers might include "It tastes bad" or "I can't swallow the pill." However, if your child says, "I don't know," you can provide scaffolding by offering suggestions like this: "Some kids don't want to take their medicine because it tastes bad. Is that it?" When the child lets you know you have pinpointed his or her concern, sum it up with another reflective response like "You're not taking your medicine because it tastes bad. Right?" This provides an opportunity for your child to correct misunderstandings.

## Step 2: Defining the Problem

When the child's concern has been acknowledged, it is time for the parents to put *their* concern on the table. Being specific in describing your concerns is just as important as being specific in identifying the child's concern. Greene and Ablon's example illustrates this point.[27]

> Parent: "I've noticed that homework has been a struggle lately. What's up?"
> Child: "I don't want to do it right after school." (Too vague.)
> Parent: "You don't want to do it right after school. How come?"
> Child: "Because I'm tired. I need a break."
> Parent: "So you don't want to do your homework right after school because you're tired and you need a break. Is that right?"
> Child: "That's right!"
> Parent: "I'm not saying you have to do your homework right after school, but I'm concerned that if you don't do it then, it won't get done." (Parent defines her concern.)

Probably the biggest stumbling block to defining the problem is the tendency for both the parent and the child to offer their solutions first. For example, "You're doing homework right after school because that's the best time!"

Initially, you want to make sure you are only stating your *concern*— not your *solution*.

## Step 3: The Invitation

The third step in collaborative problem solving is inviting the child to brainstorm ideas for solving the problem in a way that is *feasible* and *mutually satisfactory*.[28] The invitation makes it clear that you believe solving the problem is something you and your child should do together. The key word in issuing the invitation is *Let's*, as in, "Let's see what we can do about that." You can take the issue a step further and restate the concerns of both the child and the parent. ("Let's think about how we can make sure you get your homework done without your having to do it right after school.")

At this point, you and your child can brainstorm solutions that address both of your concerns. Give your child the first crack at coming up with a suggestion, and treat your kids' ideas with respect. There are no such things as *bad* solutions—only solutions that are not feasible or mutually satisfactory. Simply say, "Well, that's an idea, but as I think about it, that solution might work well for you but it wouldn't work so well for me. Let's try to think of a solution that would work well for both of us." Coming up with solutions is difficult for some kids. You can scaffold by tentatively suggesting some solutions by saying, "Well, here's a possibility ... Let me know what you think of this idea."

The very act of engaging our kids in problem solving trains them in many important skills. When parents help a child define a problem, reflect on possible solutions and outcomes, and use abstract thinking to predict the outcomes of different solutions, they are teaching their kids a more organized and rational way of thinking. This is an important stepping-stone toward maturity.

## Bringing It Home

Proverbs 20:5 says, "The purposes of a man's heart are deep waters, but a man of understanding draws them out." Unfortunately, being an understanding person is difficult when we are addressing poor behavior. We have a tendency to argue about the facts of the situation, but the root of conflict goes deeper. Conflict usually springs up because a person is trying to protect a sense of competence, value, or worth. When we see conflict as a unique opportunity to uncover these deeper issues, we can be more understanding in the midst of strong emotions. This will require putting the desire to defend *our* sense of competence on hold as we extend empathy to our children during this vulnerable time. But in doing so, we provide a safer place for our children to address the fears and insecurities that lead to their poor choice in the first place.

Having some tools for addressing poor behavior with an empathetic attitude can be helpful. The three components of assertion statements can help us maintain this delicate balance: a nonjudgmental description of the behavior, a description of the parent's feelings, and the resulting effect on the parent of the child's actions. We need to be prepared for a defensive response from our children and to meet the response with reflective listening. This greatly increases the odds that we will hear our children and that they will hear our concerns as well.

Collaborative problem solving gives parents another tool for addressing conflict. When we take time to reflect our child's concern, state our own concern, and invite them to brainstorm solutions, we are more likely to avoid the cycle of escalating emotions that often derail communication.

Our ultimate goal is to glorify God by mirroring His balance of truth and love. When we handle conflict well, we provide an example of godly love that draws our children into authentic relationship. Because relationship is the heart of the gospel message, extending love and respect to our children should always be our main goal when addressing their poor choices.

# CHAPTER 16

# THE PRODIGAL'S FATHER

We've seen how our parents have impacted our parenting styles as we imitate them or resolve to do things differently. And we've seen that in all our efforts to adapt and become the kind of parents our children need, our parenting style can become a little scattered. We need a guide—a prototypical parent we can look to as the standard. There's only been one perfect parent, and we've seen how He teaches us, using a perfect expression of the three E's of parenting—experience, example, and exploration. He sets wide boundaries for us, allows us to choose within those boundaries, and delivers consequences when we choose outside the boundaries. But He is always empathetic, forgiving our rebellion and giving us countless opportunities to try and try again. He faces our issues and walks through the consequences as our trusted counselor, not our adversary. He is always on our side, helping us learn the lessons that will transform us into the people He has designed us to be.

One of the best pictures of the perfect parent in Scripture is the story of the prodigal son (Luke 15:11–32). This story took on special meaning to us when our son went to his second treatment program. It felt like our story. And it is a great example of the parenting style we all should try to adopt.

The story is familiar to many. The father, who represented God, had two sons: an older one who was externally compliant and followed all the rules and a younger, rebellious one who was determined to rid himself of his father's authority and be his own boss.

The younger son, tired of his father's authority, approached the father and demanded his inheritance. An inheritance isn't due until death, so the son was essentially saying he wished his father was dead. In the culture of the time, this request was a major insult to the father, and the community would have been utterly shocked to hear a son say something like that to his dad.

The father's response is interesting. He had the right to severely discipline the son and even disinherit him. The father could have lectured the son on the value of family, worked him harder than ever, or rebuked him for his insulting behavior. The father could have given the son all the reasons why he wasn't ready for freedom and told him all the bad things that could happen if he tried to make it on his own. The father could have begged the son to change his mind, pleaded with him to stay, or tried to bribe him to stay with promises of greater favors. Instead, the father sold the family farm and gave each son his share. No lecture, no scolding, no pleading, and no whining.

Why wasn't the father stricter with the younger son? He could have insisted on "first-time obedience," but he didn't. He was remarkably silent with respect to all the implications of complying with the son's demand, not the least of which was damage to the father's reputation. Why? The answer seems clear: the father knew his son. He also knew his son would learn best from the experiences and the consequences of his poor choices. The father was willing to suffer a loss of respect and status in his community to allow his son to pursue a terrible course of action so the boy would learn a lesson he truly would never forget. Isn't that the way God works? He allows us to make lots of choices, many of which He knows are poor, without intervening. Then He walks with us through the consequences of those poor choices. He knows we learn best from reaping what we sow.

The rebellious younger son took the money and ran to a distant country, far from his father's watchful eye. He lived with only his own immature conscience as his guide and got into a lot of trouble. He ran out of money, and his so-called friends deserted him. Without the inheritance money, he had to find a job to survive, and he took the only job he could find: on a pig farm.

There must have been an audible gasp among the Jewish people listening to this parable when they heard the boy was working with pigs, because these animals were strictly off limits to them. Even worse, the area in which the boy lived and worked was struck with a famine. Debased and starving, the boy was reaping what he had sown in his rebellion against his father. When the father first allowed his son to leave, he must have known these difficult situations were possible and even likely to happen. Yet he was willing to let the consequences play out for the greater good of his son. Letting his son make his choices and learn from the consequences was the most loving thing the father could have done for his son because this son could learn no other way. To the people of the father's community, he must have seemed crazy and irresponsible for choosing this path.

This may happen in your lives too. People may say your job as a parent is to protect and rescue your kids from pain, and that the consequences of really poor choices are more than a child can bear. These people will expect you to bail your kids out when they get in trouble and to pull all the necessary strings to get them headed in the right direction. They will expect you to push them into the right schools, the popular sports, and the best careers. They will imply that any misstep along the way should be carefully guarded against and hidden, if possible. They may talk behind your back and even ostracize you if you choose to parent your kids the way the father in this story did. And you will have a choice: to follow the prodigal's father's lead or to follow the culture, knowing the culture will punish you for not toeing the line.

Let's see what happened for the father who chose the countercultural way to parent his son.

The prodigal son found himself wallowing in mud—hungry, lonely, and in despair. At that point, he had an epiphany. The consequences taught him a lesson he clearly could not have learned any other way, and he realized how foolish he had been. He knew he had to go back home. The once rebellious son decided to return to his father, but with no expectation of returning as a son. The son thought he could save face by asking to be a hired man rather than a restored son. After all, contractors had plenty to eat and were able to maintain some semblance of independence. We aren't sure at this point if the boy had learned everything he should have learned, but he was at least willing to return humbly and ask for restoration.

The son's resolve to maintain any sense of independence was melted by the father's response to the return of his long lost son. The father saw him from a long way off, which tells us the father had been looking for him for a long time. The neighboring farming community probably would have reported that the son had been spotted on his way toward the village and they must have been intensely interested to see this boy get his comeuppance. They had to have been immensely disappointed by the father's response. Rather than waiting on his porch for the son to reach out and beg forgiveness, the father did the unthinkable. He picked up his robe and ran to the boy, showering him in kisses. There was no, "I told you so," no scolding, no sarcastic recitation of the misfortunes of the son. Only a perfect display of unconditional love that softened the boy's heart. The son didn't even bother to ask for a job. He knew in that moment that his father welcomed him back to the family as a son. Best of all, he realized he was forgiven. His past would not be held against him but instead it would form an important part of his future as a humble, obedient son of a father who cared for him so deeply he willingly gave up his dignity and reputation so his son would have this awesome opportunity to become the man his father always knew he could be.

Just as God clothed Adam and Eve with animal skins to cover their shame, the father threw a robe around this dirty, disheveled rebel and treated him as a cherished son. He threw a party for him and made sure everyone knew his son had returned. That's empathy! The father allowed his son to experience the painful consequences of his bad choices, but he never stopped loving him.

You may be thinking about the older brother, and it seems many of us have overlooked what we can learn about parenting from the older, compliant son. Apparently, he was a rule follower and a people pleaser. He did what his father told him to do. His behavior appeared to be exemplary. But those are externals; they did not reveal his heart. Much more telling is his reaction to the return of his wayward brother. Rather than joy at the restoration of his brother, he exhibited contempt. "Look! All these years I've been slaving for you and never disobeyed your orders. Yet you never gave me even a young goat so I could celebrate with my friends. But when this son of yours who has squandered your property with prostitutes comes home, you kill the fattened calf for him!" (Luke 15:29–30).

Obviously, the older brother's compliant behavior masked a self-centered heart. He didn't obey his father out of love; he did it in order to earn his way to the favored position in the household. When some of the results of his hard work went to the rebellious brother, his entitled attitude spilled out. He felt he had earned the right to the family farm. He had been the one to work and toil when the younger son went off to waste his money. He worked to obligate his father to give him his due, not because he loved and respected him.

We don't know the end of the story, particularly with the older brother. But what we see is the love of a father who reaches out to each child with unconditional love, offering all he has without reserve. He allows his boys to have the opportunity to learn from experience and consequences, and he trusts those experiences to teach. His goal is heart change and the restoration of the relationship with his son.

## Bringing It Home

The story of the prodigal son provides an excellent example of the overarching message we see in the Bible from Genesis to Revelation. God is passionately pursuing a relationship with us. Reading His Word as both a child and a parent, we begin to understand that relationships are the keys to life.

In that context, God's "rules" make sense. He knows our relationships will suffer without them.

"Train up a child in the way he should go" (Prov. 22:6).

"Do not let unwholesome talk come out of your mouth" (Eph. 4:29).

"Do everything without complaining or arguing" (Phil. 2:14).

"Honor your father and mother" (Ex. 20:12).

Unfortunately, sometimes we get so preoccupied with making our kids obey the rules that we lose sight of why God made them in the first place. In our zeal to force our kids to comply, we end up breaking some of God's other rules.

> "A gentle answer turns away wrath, but a harsh word stirs up anger" (Prov. 15:1).

> "Everyone should be quick to listen, slow to speak and slow to become angry, for man's anger does not bring about the righteous life that God desires" (James 1:19–20).

> "Fathers, do not exasperate your children, so that they will not lose heart" (Col. 3:21, NASB).

> "A man of knowledge uses words with restraint, and a man of understanding is even-tempered" (Prov. 17:27).

When your son complains or argues, you *could* quote Philippians 2:14—"Do everything without complaining or arguing"—and insist that he stops. Ironically, you may end up complaining about his attitude and violating the same principle. Obedience based on a set of rules may change behavior, but it will rarely change the heart. Like the Pharisees who rebuked Jesus for healing on the Sabbath, we can get caught up in details and lose sight of the bigger point God is making.

Heartfelt obedience is only possible in response to a loving relationship. That is why we desire to be more Christlike—because we are responding to His love for us. God wants our earthly relationships to mirror His relationship with us. When we approach our children with this goal in mind, we truly honor Him.

Parenting is one of the most challenging responsibilities a human can have, but God's heart is deeply invested in it. Every step of the way, turn to Him as an example and a source of help. Pray for your children, pray for insight to deal with them in godly and effective ways, and pray for strength.

In His strength, you can be the parent He designed you to be.

# APPENDIX

# CONSEQUENCE WORKSHEETS

## Imaginative Consequences

If you agree that the consequences of your child's choices are great tools for learning, it makes sense you should be imaginative with the consequences you deliver rather than defaulting to the same old consequence every time (e.g., grounding). The best consequences are

a.  related to the choice made,
b.  reasonable in duration and severity for the choice made,
c.  designed to model how the consequence of a particular choice will affect the child's life when he or she has left home, and
d.  created to teach great lessons that can be applied in many situations in the real world. Each child is different, and the consequences that work for one may not be effective for another, so think about each child separately and complete a worksheet for each.

Four different types of consequence categories are listed below. Most children respond well to consequences that require them to do something for the family or another person, as opposed to taking things away. Think about each category, whether consequences under that category will be effective for each of your children, and if so, under what circumstances. Complete a worksheet for each child.

**Child's name:** _____

| Things your child does not like to do but that have to be done by someone | Things your child likes to do but are not required | Things you do as favors (not the things you normally do as a parent) | Things that can be exchanged for your time, effort, and money |
|---|---|---|---|
| Ex: Doing laundry, dusting, making beds, extra chores | Ex: Computer games, cell phone, TV | Ex: Stop for snacks on the way home from school | Ex: Because you made the bed for your child, he can make your bed the next morning |

**Child's name:** _____

| Things your child does not like to do but that have to be done by someone | Things your child likes to do but are not required | Things you do as favors (not the things you normally do as a parent) | Things that can be exchanged for your time, effort, and money |
|---|---|---|---|
| | | | |

**Child's name:** _____

| Things your child does not like to do but that have to be done by someone | Things your child likes to do but are not required | Things you do as favors (not the things you normally do as a parent) | Things that can be exchanged for your time, effort, and money |
|---|---|---|---|
| | | | |

# ENDNOTES

1. Tim Kimmel, *Raising Kids for True Greatness* (Nashville: W Publishing Group, 2006).
2. Ibid.
3. Edward Teyber, *Interpersonal Process in Therapy: An Integrative Model*, 5th ed. (Belmont, California: Thomson Brooks/Cole, 2006), 227.
4. Ibid.
5. Ibid., 218.
6. Ibid., 222.
7. Ibid.
8. Michael Valpy, "Please Excuse the Mess," *The Globe and Mail*, May 10, 2003.
9. Marco Iacoboni, "Imitation, Empathy, and Mirror Neurons," *Annual Review of Psychology* 60: (2009) 653–70.
10. John W. Santrock, *Life-Span Development*, 9th ed. (New York: McGraw Hill, 2004), 253.
11. "Inside the Teenage Brain: How Much Do We Really Know about the Brain?" *Frontline*, 2002, 6.
12. Ibid.

13. Valpy, "Please Excuse the Mess."

14. Randall Parker, "Adolescent Emotions Less Developed Than Adults," *FuturePundit,* September 10, 2006, http://www.futurepundit.com/archives/003712.html.

15. Misia Landau, "Deciphering the Adolescent Brain," *Focus,* April 21, 2000, http://archives.focus.hms.harvard.edu/2000/Apr21_2000/psychiatry.html.

16. Paul W. Brown and Herbert M. Jenkins, "Auto-Shaping of the Pigeon's Key-Peck," *Journal of the Experimental Analysis of Behavior* 11:1 (1968), 1–8.

17. Teyber, *Interpersonal Process in Therapy,* 224–30.

18. Ibid., 231.

19. Robert Bolton, *People Skills: How to Assert Yourself, Listen to Others, and Resolve Conflicts* (New York: Simon & Schuster, 1979), 15.

20. Adele Faber and Elaine Mazlish, *Liberated Parents, Liberated Children* (New York: HarperCollins Publishers, 1990), 22.

21. Bolton, *People Skills,* 217.

22. Ibid., 140.

23. Ibid., 146.

24. Ibid., 154.

25. Ibid., 160.

26. Ibid., 167.

27. Ross W. Greene and J. Stuart Ablon, *Treating Explosive Kids: The Collaborative Problem-Solving Approach* (New York: Guilford Press, 2006), 56.

28. Ibid., 59.

30832477R00139

Made in the USA
San Bernardino, CA
23 February 2016